NORO

NORO

MEET THE MAN BEHIND THE LEGENDARY YARN
KNIT 40 FABULOUS DESIGNS

CORNELIA TUTTLE HAMILTON

sixth&spring books

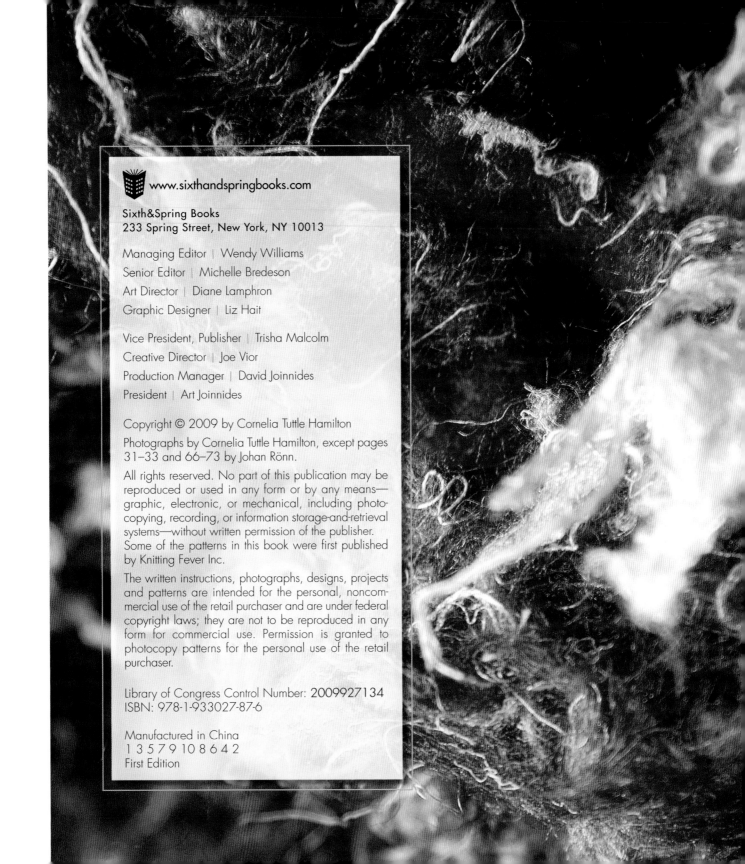

www.sixthandspringbooks.com

Sixth&Spring Books
233 Spring Street, New York, NY 10013

Managing Editor | Wendy Williams
Senior Editor | Michelle Bredeson
Art Director | Diane Lamphron
Graphic Designer | Liz Hait

Vice President, Publisher | Trisha Malcolm
Creative Director | Joe Vior
Production Manager | David Joinnides
President | Art Joinnides

Library of Congress Control Number: 2009927134
ISBN: 978-1-933027-87-6

Manufactured in China
1 3 5 7 9 10 8 6 4 2
First Edition

[Contents

野呂

Acknowledgments

Designing handknits is a creative process. Designing books, yet another.

First, my warm and fond thanks to Trisha Malcolm, vice president of Soho Publishing and publisher of Sixth&Spring Books, for making this book possible. Many thanks to editors Michelle Bredeson and Wendy Williams for holding the reins of this project and keeping track of everything—including me, at times. Thanks to all the other people at Sixth&Spring Books involved in the creation of this book.

Thanks to my assistant, Madeleine Malmberg.

Much love and thanks to my family and friends who have supported my efforts over the years.

Last, and perhaps most importantly, a special thanks to Mr. Eisaku Noro for producing the yarns all these years that have inspired me like no other yarns.

This book is dedicated to Noro lovers everywhere!

Introduction

My relationship with all that is Noro began in the early 1980s. I had just returned from a train trip around Europe that I undertook to find direction in my professional life. The outcome was an ambitious decision to pursue careers in both photography and hand-knit design. As fate would have it, the design part of my decision quickly developed and pushed out the photography—at least for the time being.

Upon my return to Manhattan I took a sales job at Fiberworks, which was probably the most avant-garde yarn shop in New York at the time. Owned by crochet designer Judith Copeland, Fiberworks was more a gallery than a yarn shop, where handcrafted yarns from Noro lit up the shelves and were featured in artfully displayed hand-knit garments.

It was quite clear to me from the start that the yarns produced by Noro were in a category all their own—vibrantly colorful, wonderfully textural and excitingly different from all other yarns on offer. They quickly became my favorites to look at and knit with. And so they have remained ever since.

For the past five years, it has been my great fortune to be able to give form to the wonderful yarns from Noro. For that I have Sion Elalouf at Knitting Fever, Inc., to thank. He asked me create a book of hand knits using Noro yarns, and, needless to say, I jumped at the chance. One book was followed by four more in as many years.

It has been a rare privilege to work with these beautiful yarns in the expression of my creativity. That experience would in itself be gratifying enough for me, but to finally meet Eisaku Noro himself was equally rewarding and a longtime dream come true.

It is my pleasure to share with you what I learned about Eisaku Noro and his company during my visit to Japan in the early spring of 2008. You will also find forty of my most popular designs that feature Noro yarns. I hope that working with these remarkable yarns will give you as much pleasure and inspiration as it has given me.

Noro: An Inside Look

The gratification of working with the ever-changing yarns from Noro has undeniably been one of the greatest joys of my career. These yarns have accompanied me throughout the past 25 years, marking changes in season, fashion and my own personal evolution as a designer. Each successive collection has brought with it the excitement of new and often unexpected fiber combinations, textures and colorways. Noro yarns are always well designed and different from all other yarns on the market.

For me, it doesn't get better than designing with Noro yarns. It's a joy to explore the characteristics of each new yarn and figure out ways of showcasing its individual personality. To design in these yarns and not take into account their intrinsic characteristics, what I call the "ego" of each yarn, is to not fully acknowledge the brilliance of their development.

I have come to believe that these yarns are as close to art as we have in the industry. The man behind them is an artist himself, and these yarns are an expression of his spirit rather than just a commercial product. So much thought, skill and passion are behind the development of these beautiful yarns. I have learned over the years that there is a purpose behind the characteristics of each specific yarn. If one is rustic and somewhat rough to the touch with vivid, sometimes clashing colors, well, that's exactly how Eisaku Noro wants it to be! Likewise if a yarn is soft and earth-toned. For the past three decades, Noro has succeeded through his products in mesmerizing his audience more completely than anyone else in the industry.

Even after working with Noro yarns and designing five books of designs featuring them, I still had not met the man behind the yarns! Not from lack of curiosity, mind you, but Japan is a long way from Sweden (my home since 1986), and the

The spun yarn ready to be wound into skeins or hanks.

Mr. Eisaku Noro—then and now.

opportunity did not arise until I was doing research for this book. Over time and through working with his yarns, I had developed my own idea about Eisaku Noro. I hadn't realized how specific it was until it came time for my trip to Japan. It was only then that I began to entertain the possibility that perhaps the image that I had built up of this person might differ from the reality.

So it was with great anticipation, excitement and a sense of privilege that I embarked on the long journey to Japan in March of 2008, for the purpose of meeting the legendary Eisaku Noro and learning more about him and his life's work.

The Man Behind the Yarns

The only picture I had ever seen of Eisaku Noro was a black-and-white photo taken roughly 35 years ago. I have looked at that portrait many times over the years, searching the features for some insight into the mind of the man behind the yarns. To my eye, he hasn't changed much from that photo; he is still trim, handsome and casually elegant. He is a simple, very focused man. A man at ease with himself and with others; a satisfied man still at the peak of his senses. He is humble, gracious, generous and full of humor—a thinker, a doer, an artist. For me, meeting him was an inspiration and a confirmation of the image of him that had taken shape over the years through working with his yarns.

Now 70, Eisaku Noro stays fit by walking an hour in the morning and again in the evening, through his interest in organic Japanese food and through his continued passion for his work, which is his life. I get the feeling that this is a man who will be working until he takes his last breath. It is obvious that every new day still brings new discoveries of color and form based largely on an acute observation of nature and its rhythms, seasons, textures and colors. Mr. Noro's calm dignity and humor were evident even though we needed an interpreter to communicate.

The Company

The Noro offices are in a low unpretentious building in the town of Ichinomiya in Central Japan—a region known for its yarn and textile production. It is where Eisaku Noro was raised. Impatient with school, Noro began working in the yarn industry after his basic education in spinning and dyeing was completed. He quickly learned the ropes. An innovator with an artistic eye even back then, Noro soon became frustrated with the constraints of working for someone else and, at age 30, branched out on his own. He named the line "The World of Nature," and that name is still printed on the label of every ball of yarn. An earnest feeling for the purity in and preservation of nature has been part of the Noro philosophy from the start.

I quickly realized that there has been virtually no deviation from the original spark that led Eisaku Noro to start his own company to actualize his ideas about making yarns. This is all the more remarkable, I now realize, against the backdrop of this conservative and tradition-steeped culture. Right from the outset, he incorporated his reverence for

Noro: An Inside Look continued

 There is a sense of joy and ease among the employees, some of whom...have been with the company for over 25 years.

nature and his artistic sensibilities into the yarn he was producing, the likes of which had never been seen before. By specially adapting industrial carding and spinning machines, Eisaku Noro was able to produce yarns that were totally unique and that put much less strain on the environment than is usual in the industry. The yarns were very colorful and ahead of their time. And they were not easy to sell. In fact, they were deemed by many as unsellable! They were simply too different from what people were accustomed to.

Several years after his company was founded, Noro met Sion Elalouf, who had seen the Noro yarns at a trade show in Asia. Elalouf was laying the foundation for his own company, Knitting Fever, Inc., in the United States, and he immediately recognized the uniqueness of the product and the potential for selling Noro yarns on the North American market. The two men have been successfully doing business together ever since.

Although in North America Noro yarns are mostly identified with hand-knitting, Noro has put extensive development into producing felted fabrics. The company also makes yarns used only in the production of ready-to-wear clothing. The yarns have not escaped the interest of felting artists, who appreciate the brilliance the colors and textures lend to their forms. About 30 percent of Noro's hand-

knitting yarns are sold in some 200 yarn shops in Japan. The rest is exported throughout the world.

The Noro offices are humble by Western standards. There are no private workspaces in the low-slung building; everyone has his or her own desk and works in the same big, rectangular room. Mr. Noro's desk is all the way in the back corner and is very neat. There are several work tables for the perusal of yarns and materials, and there is a small sitting area by the entrance with a low table and chairs for meetings with clients. Knitting swatches hang along the walls, and sample garments are piled here and there near house designer Asaku Ishii's work area. Spools, hanks, balls and cones of sample yarn are in another part of the room. This is a workplace full of color and creative disarray. I might have visited too early to witness the beauty of the Japanese cherry blossoms, but the explosion of color that I encountered at the Noro offices was distinctly satisfying!

I had the honor of meeting several key members of Noro's staff. There is a sense of joy and ease among the employees, some of whom, like Asaku Ishii, have been with the company for over 25 years.

After visiting the main floor, I climbed a rickety ladder to the second floor where the color workshop is located. It is a tiny room in which the color combinations that Noro is so famous for are

1 *Kureyon* color swatches. 2 Noro designer Junko Isaji. 3 Design samples. 4 Pattern swatches showcase the characteristics of various Noro yarns. 5 From left to right: Noriko Yamada, who works in product development; Michiko Noda, translator; Ai Muramoto, who is in charge of environmental protection. 6 More pattern swatches! 7 The company archives. 8 Noriko, planning the next season's colorways.

野呂 Dyed wool tufts used for creating the celebrated Noro colorways fill the color room.

Noro yarns have always been at the forefront of the green movement, providing us with eco-friendly options since almost before the term eco-friendly was coined.

born. Shelves stuffed with folders fill the walls. The tables are covered with tufts of yarn in every color imaginable. The designers carefully choose from these tufts and arrange them on large sheets of stiff paper. The chosen shades will become the next season's colorways for each different yarn. I mentioned to Noriko Yamada that I had some old Noro yarns in my stash, and she was curious. She asked if I could send her pictures and samples. I wondered if it was possible that they might not have any routine for the documenting of yarns from years gone by. But somehow this would not surprise me. I can relate to the habit of moving steadily forward, thinking you will document thoroughly and never quite getting around to it. Perhaps since there is no fear of lack of ideas, the focus is on moving forward. I promised to send her pictures and clippings of the yarns that I had.

The World of Nature

In recent years, the yarn industry has been actively promoting awareness of ecological sustainability, but this concept has been part of the Noro philosophy from the beginning. Noro yarns have always been at the forefront of the green movement, providing us with eco-friendly options since almost

before the term eco-friendly was coined. The preservation of nature is such an important part of his business that Mr. Noro leaves nothing to chance and personally oversees every aspect of production from sheep to yarn ball, including all machinery, labeling, yarn bags, boxes and even the garbage that the company produces. There are restrictions in the dyeing process to keep things environmentally friendly. For example, deep colors and black are often created by blending different colored fibers. Quoting Mr. Noro, "Eco certification should not be bought. It should be an integral part of every business."

All the animal fibers used in the yarns are organic. The farms they come from are certified, and the fibers are stringently checked for authenticity at all stages of their journey from the animal to Japan. Most of the wool fibers come from a special breed of sheep called Polwarth, which is raised especially for Noro on a farm in Australia. There is no mulesing (a controversial practice in which strips of skin are removed from around a sheep's buttocks to prevent infestation by flies), no unnecessary medicines are administered and the sheep have their own drinking ponds. Noro checks the water and soil on the farm, the sheep's food and the

Noro: An Inside Look continued

 The feeling of urgency common to industrial production is absent. There is no question that the production going on here is actually a form of handcrafting—there is nothing much industrial about it at all.

chemicals used in washing the wool. The company also conducts yarn analyses. Noro also gets some of its raw materials from other sources, including wool from the Falkland Islands and kid mohair from South Africa. And so on. All fiber sources are carefully researched, vetted and certified. The fibers are then freighted to Japan and checked again before being turned into the wonderful yarns that bear the Noro name.

The Production Process

The Noro company has been eco-friendly for over 30 years. In addition to using raw materials that are ecologically produced, the production of the yarns is geared to environmental preservation. Perhaps the greatest innovation is that the process of creating yarn has been shortened through unique developments by Eisaku Noro himself in the manufacturing machinery. These developments are not only beneficial from an environmental standpoint, but are also responsible for giving Noro yarns their unique handcrafted quality.

I asked Mr. Noro why he developed this new method of production. He replied, "Friction, rubbing and heat during processing weaken the fibers in direct proportion to the length of time they are processed. By dramatically shortening this process we are preventing damage to the enzymes in the

fibers and simultaneously profiting the environment."

Environmental considerations are in the forefront in the dyeing process, and each step is carefully controlled. The natural fibers are dyed using reactive and acid dyes at cool temperatures and with a ph balance that is compatible with the fibers. Nylon is colored with acid dyes and partially reactive dyes.

It was now time to walk to one of the plants and see the actual production of the yarns. The first area we entered had a big, heavy blower in it. There were bags of vibrantly dyed, semi-matted fiber tufts. Some were wool, some wool and silk, some wool and nylon. These tufts are moistened and then hand-fed into the blower which separates, loosens and mixes the fibers to facilitate the carding process. The fibers are blown into a panelled room, and there are gathered into large bags. These bags are then carried over to the carding area.

The main part of the plant is dimly lit, perhaps to save energy, making picture-taking a challenge. There is a serenity here, but also a sense of purpose. The feeling of urgency common to industrial production is absent. There is no question that the production going on here is actually a form of handcrafting—there is nothing much industrial about it at all.

We climbed atop the carding machine. Normally this machine would have three big rollers, but Noro

1 Rows of dyed fibers. 2 Dyed fibers are moistened before they go into the blower. 3 Fibers fly in the air of the blowing room. 4 Fibers are weighed and arranged according to color scheme before carding. 5 and 6 The carding machine. 7 Spools of carded fibers. 8 The spools are stored on racks to await spinning. 9 and 10 Close-ups of carded fibers. 11 The spinning machine. 12 Fibers being spun—the last step to becoming Noro yarn.

1 Shelves filled with sample garments provide a colorful backdrop in the showroom. 2 Freshly spun *Iro* yarn.
3 and 4 Spools of colorful carded fibers await spinning. 5 *Kureyon* yarn—ready for knitting!

Within the macrocosm of Japanese culture, the Noro company can be seen as a microcosm with its own traditions and values.

uses only one, which shortens the carding process and lends more variation to the final thickness of the yarn. The fibers are weighed and the colors are arranged by hand according to designated specifications. The fibers are then aligned and slowly fed into the carding machine. Carding produces a strand of yarn that is not yet twisted. The machine works at a deliberate pace, and the gauzy strands that are produced are slowly rolled onto big spools. These beautiful spools are stored on racks until the yarn is ready to be spun.

Next to the carding machine is a long spinning machine called a mule. It runs smoothly, the strands gently twisting back onto themselves on wooden pins. The rhythm of the spinning machine is mesmerizing, almost hypnotic. The bed of the machine has been shortened to create less twist in the one-ply yarns. It is old and boasts the beautiful oiled patina that wood acquires after many years of careful use.

The yarns are then transported to another plant close by, where they are steamed to set the twist, put up into skeins or hanks, and carefully labeled and bagged.

Noro's modifications to the blowing, carding and spinning processes reaps a total energy savings of 46 percent as compared to typical yarn industry standards. Because of these adjustments to the process, the plant is less dusty, less noisy and

has less chemical smell than is usually found in a yarn manufacturing plant. No waste is generated.

Years ago I came to regard each skein of Noro yarn as an individual. They are all different. Now I can really understand why. Having seen how the yarns are produced has only deepened my respect for Noro yarns.

The Future of Noro

While still very much at the forefront of running his company, it is clear that Mr. Noro's aim is to keep the business prospering even after he has passed the reins to his son, Takuo Noro, who has been working in the Noro company as operations manager for more than a decade. This seems as natural to him as the environmental sustainability of the products and the endurance of the philosophy and work ethic that he has created. There is a tangible pride among the Noro employees and a respect for their workplace and purpose.

Within the macrocosm of Japanese culture, the Noro company can be seen as a microcosm with its own traditions and values. Undeniably the manifestation of one man's spirit, the company has sprouted from the old but not broken with it, providing instead a sense of continuity between what has been and what will be in the ongoing evolution of Japanese culture. ■

Jacaranda Wrap Top

My inspiration for this shapely top was an ordinary envelope. The back is straight and the shaping is produced by wrapping and tying the front pieces around the body. The body is knit in *Blossom*, and the edging is knit in *Cash Iroha*.

Sizes
S (M, L)

Finished Measurements
▥ Bust approx 33 (35½, 38)"/84 (90, 96.5)cm
▥ Length approx 25½ (26¼, 27)"/65 (66.5, 68.5)cm

Yarn
200 (250, 300)g *Blossom* #06
50 (50, 50)g *Cash Iroha* #111

Needles
One pair each size 9 and 11 (5.5 and 7mm) straight needles *or size to obtain gauge*

Gauges
12 sts/24 rows = 4"/10cm with *Blossom* and size 11 (7mm) needles in Gst
15 sts/21 rows = 4"/10cm with *Cash Iroha* and size 9 (5.5mm) needles in St st
Take time to check gauge.

NOTES
▥ The edging will naturally roll to the inside, so no additional finishing is necessary.
▥ Make sure to bind off edging loosely or it will pull together and cause the fabric to pucker.
▥ If you have trouble locating *Blossom*, this pattern can be knit in *Kochoran* using the same amount of yarn and size needles.

I-CORD TIE
Cast on 4 sts.
Row 1 Knit.
Row 2 Slip all sts.

BACK

With *Blossom* and size 11 (7mm) needles, cast on 72 (74, 76) sts and work Gst for 14½ (15¾, 17)"/37 (40, 43)cm. Bind off all sts over next row.

RIGHT FRONT

With *Blossom* and size 11 (7mm) needles, cast on 48 (49, 50) sts and work Gst for 12 (12, 12) rows.

▓ Armhole

Next row (RS) At end of row, with *Blossom* and size 11 (7mm) needles, cast on 24 (25, 26) sts. Cont in Gst over all sts until piece measures 3¼ (4, 4¾)"/8 (10, 12)cm, ending with a RS row.

▓ Front shaping

Next row (WS at top of Right Front) Bind off 2 sts at beg of every other row as follows: Slip edge st, k1, psso, bind off 1 st. Work to end.

Next row (RS at bottom of Right Front) Bind off 1 st beg of every other row as follows: Slip edge st, k1, psso. Work to end.

Work decs until there are no more sts. Fasten off. This is the waist point.

LEFT FRONT

With *Blossom* and size 11 (7mm) needles, cast on and work as for Right Front, reversing the shaping.

EDGINGS AND FINISHING

Right Front

With *Cash Iroha*, size 9 (5.5mm) needles and RS facing, beg at the bottom side edge pick up 56 (58, 60) sts to waist point, work 1 st in the point, and cont to pick up 70 (72, 74) sts to shoulder edge. Work 4 rows in St st starting with a knit row. *At same time:* On knit rows, work one inc at each side of center point st, 2 times. Bind off all sts loosely over next row.

Left Front

With *Cash Iroha*, size 9 (5.5 mm) needles and RS facing, beg at the shoulder edge pick up 70 (72, 74) sts to waist point, work 1 st in the point, and cont to pick up 56 (58, 60) sts to bottom side edge. Work 4 rows in St st starting with a knit row. *At same time:* On knit rows, work one inc of each side of center point st, 2 times. Bind off all sts loosely over next row.

Join shoulder seams.

Back Neck

With *Cash Iroha*, size 9 (5.5 mm) needles and RS facing, pick up 45 (45, 45) sts across back neck. Work 4 rows in St st starting with a knit row. Bind off all sts loosely over next row.

Armhole Edging

With *Cash Iroha*, size 9 (5.5 mm) needles and RS facing, pick up 58 (62, 66) sts evenly spaced around armhole edge. Work 4 rows in St st, starting with a knit row. Bind off all sts loosely over next row.

Bottom of Back

With *Cash Iroha*, size 9 (5.5 mm) needles and RS facing, pick up 56 (58, 60) sts evenly spaced along bottom of Back. Work 4 rows in St st, starting with a knit row. Bind off all sts loosely over next row.

Join left side seam and edging. Join right side seam and edging, leaving a 1"/2.5 cm opening at the height of the point for the tie to pass through. Join edging at shoulders.

FINISHING

Work an I-cord tie for 15"/38cm and attach to point on Right Front. Work another I-cord tie for 45"/114cm and attach to point on Left Front. ■

Benedikta Patchwork Sweater

The mitred blocks in this sweater make a raglan treatment of the sleeve and a V-neck obvious design choices. You can greatly vary the look of this piece by selecting different yarn colors. Have fun choosing a unique combination!

■ ■ ■ ■▶

Size
M/L

Finished Measurements
■ Bust 46½"/118cm
■ Length 23½"/60cm

Yarn
150g *Silk Garden Lite* #2015
100g each *Silk Garden Lite* #2010 and 2014
350g *Silk Garden Lite* #2011

Needles
One pair size 6 (4mm) straight needles
or size to obtain gauge

Gauge
20 sts = 4"/10cm in St st
Take time to check gauge.

BLOCKS
Row 1 (RS) K20 sts down right side of point, k1 st in middle, k20 sts up left side of point.
Row 2 (WS) K20, p1, k20.
Row 3 K18, k2tog tbl, sl 1 st, k2tog, k18.
Row 4 Purl.
Row 5 K17, k2tog tbl, sl 1 st, k2tog, k17.
Row 6 Purl.
Row 7 K16, k2tog tbl, sl 1 st, k2tog, k16.
Row 8 K17, p1, k17.
Row 9 K15, k2tog tbl, sl 1 st, k2tog, k15.
Row 10 Purl.
Row 11 K14, k2tog tbl, sl 1 st, k2tog, k14.
Row 12 Purl.
Row 13 K13, k2tog tbl, sl 1 st, k2tog, k13.
Row 14 K14, p1, k14.
Row 15 K12, k2tog tbl, sl 1 st, k2tog, k12.
Row 16 Purl.
Row 17 K11, k2tog tbl, sl 1 st, k2tog, k11.
Row 18 Purl.

Row 19 K10, k2tog tbl, sl 1 st, k2tog, k10.
Row 20 K11, p1, k11.
Row 21 K9, k2tog tbl, sl 1 st, k2tog, k9.
Row 22 Purl.
Row 23 K8, k2tog tbl, sl 1 st, k2tog, k8.
Row 24 Purl.
Row 25 K7, k2tog tbl, sl 1 st, k2tog, k7.
Row 26 K8, p1, k8.
Row 27 K6, k2tog tbl, sl 1 st, k2tog, k6.
Row 28 Purl.
Row 29 K5, k2tog tbl, sl 1 st, k2tog, k5.
Row 30 Purl.
Row 31 K4, k2tog tbl, sl 1 st, k2tog, k4.
Row 32 K5, p1, k5.
Row 33 K3, k2tog tbl, sl 1 st, k2tog, k3.
Row 34 Purl.
Row 35 K2, k2tog tbl, sl 1 st, k2tog, k2.
Row 36 Purl.
Row 37 K1, k2tog tbl, sl 1 st, k2tog, k1.
Row 38 K2, p1, k2.
Row 39 K2tog tbl, sl 1 st, k2tog.
Row 40 Purl.
Row 41 Sl 1, k2tog, psso. Pull yarn through rem st to fasten off.

GARTER STITCH BORDER AT BOTTOM (make 2)

With *Silk Garden Lite* #2011, cast on 129 sts and work in Gst for 3¼"/8cm.

Next row (RS) K16, *bind off 1 st, k31*, end with bind off 1 st, k16.

▦ First Point (16 sts)
Next row (WS) Knit 16 sts.
Next row (RS) *Bind off 1 st, k to end.
Rep these 2 rows until 1 st remains. There will be one fewer st on every WS row. Pull yarn through st to fasten off.

▦ Second, Third and Fourth Points (31 sts)
Next row (WS) Bind off 1 st, k30 sts. Turn.
Next row (RS) Bind off 1 st, k29 sts.
Rep these 2 rows, binding off at beg of each row until 1 st remains. Pull yarn through st to fasten off.

▦ Fifth Point (16 sts)
Next row (WS) Bind off 1 st, k to end.
Next row (RS) Knit.
Rep these 2 rows until 1 st remains. There will be one fewer st on every WS row. Pull yarn through st to fasten off.

BODY

Join side seams. Work one block between each two points, consecutively around the body.
First block row Work blocks with #2010.
Second block row Work blocks with #2015.
Third block row Work blocks with #2014.

Fourth block row Work blocks with #2011.
Fifth block row Work blocks with #2010.
Divide work at side seam. Front and Back are now worked separately.

BACK AND FRONT
The V at middle Front and Back is empty for the neck opening. The V at each armhole is also empty for raglan shaping. Work one block at each side of middle V on both Front and Back.

SLEEVES (make 2)
With *Silk Garden Lite* #2011, cast on 50 sts and work in Gst. Inc 1 st at each side every 8 rows, 18 times—86 sts. Cont to work evenly until piece measures 17¾"/45cm.

▦ Raglan Shaping
Dec 1 st at each side every other row (leaving 2 selvage sts at each side), 30 times—26 sts. Leave rem sts on a stitch holder.

NECK EDGING
Join sleeves to body. From the right shoulder and down to the middle of Back, pick up 40 sts, 1 st at middle, 40 sts along left side of Back, 26 sts from Sleeve, 40 sts along left side of Front, 1 st at middle, 40 sts up the right side of Front and 26 sts from Sleeve.
Work back and forth in Gst.

RS rows Dec on both sides of middle st of Front and Back as follows: k2tog tbl, sl 1 st,
k2tog. *At same time*: Cont to dec along sleeve edges as established.

WS rows Knit all sts except for the middle sts Front and Back, which should be purled.
Work all decs, 9 times. Now work only the decs at sides of middle sts Front and Back, 6 more times. Bind off all sts over next row.

FINISHING
Join seam of Neck Edging. Join sleeve seams. ◼

Mazatapec Hat and Scarf

The knotted fringe on this hat and scarf makes practical use of the yarn ends that are a byproduct of knitting stripes—perfect for folks who don't like finishing! Worked entirely in garter stitch, the hat is knit side to side and seamed.

Size
Adult

Finished Measurements
- Hat circumference approx 22"/56cm
- Hat height approx 10"/25.5cm
- Scarf width approx 5½"/14cm
- Scarf length approx 79"/200cm

Yarn
- Hat

50g Blossom #12
50g Cash Iroha #22

- Scarf

200g Blossom #12
150g Cash Iroha #22

Needles
One pair size 9 (6mm) straight needles
or size to obtain gauge

Gauge
13 sts/24 rows = 4"/10cm square in Gst with *Blossom*
Take time to check gauge.

NOTE
- When working *Cash Iroha* rows: At right-side edge of work (bottom of hat) save approx 2½"/6cm of yarn. At left-side edge of work (top of hat) save 6–8"/15–20cm at each turn. Do not clip.
- If you have trouble locating *Blossom*, this pattern can be knit in *Kochoran* using the same amount of yarn and size needles.

STRIPE PATTERN
Work 6 rows Gst with *Blossom*.
Work 2 rows in Gst with *Cash Iroha* held double. Save approx 2½"/6 cm of yarn at beg and end of each *Cash Iroha* row (they don't need to be cut before piece is finished).
Repeat these 8 rows throughout.

野呂 29

SCARF

With *Blossom,* cast on 18 sts. Work in Stripe pattern above until *Blossom* is almost finished. Work 6 rows in *Blossom.* Bind off all sts.

FINISHING

Tie an overhand knot at each side of rows with *Cash Iroha.* Cut ends evenly, leaving approx 1"/2.5 cm of fringe (or desired length).

HAT

With *Cash Iroha* held double, cast on 30 sts. Work Stripe pattern as follows:

Row 1 Knit.

Row 2 Knit.

Change to *Blossom.*

Row 3 K24, turn work.

Row 4 Sl 1 st with yarn at front of work, k23.

Row 5 K18, turn work.

Row 6 Sl 1 st with yarn at front of work, k17.

Row 7 Knit.

Row 8 Knit.

When piece measures 21¼"/54 cm along right-side edge, end with 6 rows of *Blossom.* Bind off all sts.

FINISHING

Join seam at back. Tie all ends at bottom edge of hat using overhand knots. Trim ends neatly to desired length. Divide the ends at top of hat and tie a knot. ■

Klaralund Kimono Sweater

The pleasing shape of this design was inspired by Japanese kimonos. The wide sleeves continue at the armholes and are joined at the middle of the front and back. The bottom is worked separately in the round.

Sizes
XS (S, S2, M, M2, L, XL)

Finished Measurements
▥ Bust 34 (36, 38, 40, 42, 44, 46)"/86.5 (91.5, 101.5, 107, 112, 117)cm
▥ Length 21½ (22, 22½, 23, 23½, 24, 24½)"/54.5 (56, 57, 58.5, 60, 61, 62)cm

Yarn
400 (450, 500, 550, 600, 650, 700)g
Silk Garden in #8

Needles
One pair size 8 (5mm) straight needles *or size to obtain gauge*
One 30"/80cm size 8 (5mm) circular needle *or size to obtain gauge*

Gauges
16 sts/22 rows = 4" in St st
16 sts/32 rows = 4" in Garter st
Take time to check gauge.

EXTENDED GARTER STITCH
Rows 1 and 3 Knit.
Row 2 Purl.
Row 4 Knit.
Repeat these 4 rows.

BOTTOM
On circular needle, cast on 136 (144, 152, 160, 168, 176, 184) sts.
Rnd 1 Knit.
Rnd 2 Purl.
Repeat these 2 rnds 7 times.
Cont now in St st until piece measures 13 (13½, 14, 14½, 15, 15½, 16)"/33 (34, 35.5, 37, 38, 39.5, 40.5)cm.
Work Rnd 2. Thereafter work Rnds 1 and 2 4 times.

At same time: Place 4 markers evenly along last round, one every 34 (36, 38, 40, 42, 44, 46) sts. These mark the Right and Left sides and center Front and Back. Bind off all sts over next row.

SLEEVE (make 2)

Cast on 60 (62, 64, 66, 66, 66, 66) sts on straight needles and work 14 rows in Gst.

Next row (RS) Change to St st, beg with a k row. Work evenly until piece measures 16½ (16½, 16½, 16, 16, 15½, 15½)"/42 (42, 42, 40.5, 40.5, 39.5, 39.5)cm, ending with a RS row.

Next row (WS) Work 9 rows in Garter st.

▥ Sleeve Tops

Change to Extended Gst and work until piece measures 25 (25½, 26, 26, 26½, 26½, 27)"/63.5 (65, 66, 66, 67, 67, 68.5)cm. Change to Gst again and work 14 rows. Bind off all sts.

FINISHING

Join side seams. Join sleeve seams from bottom for approx 18 (18, 18, 17½, 17½, 17, 17)"/46 (46, 46, 44.5, 44.5, 43. 43)cm, ending with the 9 rows of Gst to match bottom. Place right side of Right Sleeve top along bound-off edge of Bottom from center Front marker to Right Side marker. Join, easing in any extra rows from sleeve. Place left side of Right Sleeve top along bound-off edge of Bottom from Right side marker to center Back marker. Join. Repeat with Left Sleeve. At back, join the sleeve tops at bind-off edges from center of Back toward neck for 4½ (5, 5½, 6, 6, 6, 6)"/11.5 (12.5, 14, 15, 15, 15, 15)cm. ▪

野呂 33

Ekeby Vest

This vest is composed simply of garter stitch and rhythmically spaced long buttonholes. I have worked this pattern in several other yarns in different weights with less satisfying results, but *Silk Garden Chunky* will do the trick if you want to substitute.

Sizes
S/M (M/L)

Finished Measurements
▦ Bust 38(41)"/96(104)cm
▦ Length 19½(19½)"/49(49)cm

Yarn
300(400)g *Iro* in #26

Needles
One pair size 11 (8 mm) straight needles
or size to obtain gauge

Gauge
12 sts/20 rows = 4"/10 cm in Gst
Take time to check gauge.

NOTE
Check the number of sts on needle occasionally.

FRONT
Cast on 64 sts and work 3 (9) rows in Gst.

Row 1 (RS) (K4, bind off 8 sts) 5 times, end with k4. There will be 4 sts between each of 5 bound-off areas.

Row 2 (RS) (K4, cast on 8 sts) 5 times, end with k4—64 sts.

Rows 3 and 4 Knit.

Row 5 (RS) K10, (bind off 8 sts, k4) 4 times, end with k6. There will be 4 sts between each of 4 bound-off areas.

Row 6 (WS) K10, (cast on 8 sts, k4) 4 times, end with k6—64 sts.

Rows 7 and 8 Knit.

野呂

Ekeby Vest continued

Row 9 (K4, bind off 8 sts) 5 times, end with k4.

Row 10 (K4, cast on 8 sts) 5 times, end with k4.

Row 11 and 12 Knit.

Row 13 Bind off 6 sts, (k4, bind off 8 sts) 4 times, end with k10.

Row 14 K10, (cast on 8 sts, k4) 4 times, end with cast on 6 sts.

Rows 15 and 16 Knit.

Row 17 (K4, bind off 8 sts) 5 times, end with k4.

Row 18 (K4, cast on 8 sts) 5 times, end with k4.

Rows 19 and 20 Knit.

Row 21 K10, (bind off 8 sts, k4) 4 times, end with k6.

Row 22 K10, (cast on 8 sts, k4) 4 times, end with k6.

Rows 23 and 24 Knit.

Row 25 (K4, bind off 8 sts) 5 times, end with k4.

Row 26 (K4, cast on 8 sts) 5 times, end with k4.

Row 27 and 28 Knit.

Row 29 K10, (bind off 8 sts, k4) 4 times, end with bind off 6 sts. Break yarn.

Row 30 Cast on 6 sts, (k4, cast on 8 sts,) 4 times, end with k10.

Rows 31 and 32 Knit.

Row 33 (K4, bind off 8 sts) 5 times, end with k4.

Row 34 (K4, cast on 8 sts) 5 times, end with k4.

Row 35 and 36 Knit.

Row 37 K10, (bind off 8 sts, k4) 4 times, end with k6.

Row 38 K10, (cast on 8 sts, k4) 4 times, end with k6.

Row 39 and 40 Knit.

Row 41 (K4, bind off 8 sts) 5 times, end with k4.

Row 42 (K4, cast on 8 sts) 5 times, end with k4.

Rows 43 and 44 Knit.

Row 45 Bind off 6 sts, (k4, bind off 8 sts) 4 times, end with k10.

Row 46 K10, (cast on 8 sts, k4) 4 times, end with cast on 6 sts.

Rows 47 and 48 Knit.

Row 49 (K4, bind off 8 sts) 5 times, end with k4.

Row 50 (K4, cast on 8 sts) 5 times, end with k4.

Rows 51 and 52 Knit.

Row 53 K10, (bind off 8 sts, k4) 4 times, end with k6.

Row 54 K10, (cast on 8 sts, k4) 4 times, end with k6.

Rows 55 and 56 Knit.

Row 57 (K4, bind off 8 sts) 5 times, end with k4.

Row 58 (K4, cast on 8 sts) 5 times, end with k4.

Knit 3 (9) rows. Bind off all sts on next row.

BACK

Work same as for front *except for* rows 29 and 30. Work these 2 rows as follows:

Row 29 K10, (bind off 8 sts, k4) 4 times, end with k6.

Row 30 K10, (cast on 8 sts, k4) 4 times, end with k6.

FINISHING

Join 16 (25) rows at each shoulder for seam. Join side seams, leaving 9 (9½)"/22 (23)cm for armhole opening. ■

Lotorp Origami Bag

This funky shoulder bag was my first "origami" bag. Worked in one piece, it is then folded together to form the bottom. Since bags made of yarn often stretch, it's a good idea to line this one with a sturdy piece of prewashed cotton, cut out using the unfinished bag as a template.

Finished Measurements
■ Width approx 15½"/39cm wide
■ Length approx 25½"/65cm in (includes shoulder strap)

Yarn
Approx 300g *Iro* #55

Needles
One pair size 10 (6mm) straight needles
or size to obtain gauge

Gauge
Approx 16 sts/32 rows = 4"/10cm in Gst
Time time to check gauge.

NOTES
■ This pattern can also be knit in *Silk Garden Chunky* using the same amount of yarn and size needles.
■ The bag is knit tightly in one piece.
■ The size of the bag can easily be varied by using different yarns.

BAG
Cast on 14 sts and knit 1 row.
First inc row K2, m1, k to end.
Rep inc row 46 times—60 sts.
First dec row K2, k2tog, k to end.
Rep dec row 46 times—14 sts.
Second inc row K2, m1, k to end.
Rep inc row 46 times—60 sts.

Lotorp Origami Bag continued

Second dec row K2, k2tog, k to end.
Rep dec row 46 times—14 sts.
Third inc row K2, m1, k to end.
Rep inc row 46 times—60 sts.
Third dec row K2, k2tog, k to end.
Rep dec row 46 times—14 sts.
Cont to work these 14 sts in Gst for
11½"/58cm or desired length. Bind off.

FINISHING
Fold piece in half lengthwise. Fold in the
2 outer triangles to line up side edges with
the sides of the middle triangle. Join seams
on both sides of bag. Try on bag to check that
length of shoulder strap feels right. Adjust if
necessary by either adding or subtracting rows.
Join end of shoulder strap to cast-on edge. ■

I find it fascinating how the self-striping aspect of these yarns can be
used to enhance shaping as in this bag, which is knit here in *Kureyon*.

Hedvig
Rollneck Sweater

This loose-fitting top looks good on many different body types and is comfortable to wear. While the version shown here is cropped, it can also be knit long.

Sizes
S/M (M/L, L/XL)

Finished Measurements
▥ Bust 42½ (48, 53½)"/108 (122, 136)cm
▥ Length (short version) 14 (14½, 15)"/35.5 (37, 38)cm
▥ Length (long version) 19½ (20, 20½)"/49.5 (51, 52)cm

Yarn
▥ Short version
150 (200, 250)g *Silk Garden #234*
100 (100, 100)g *Cash Iroha #7*
▥ Long version
150 (200, 250)g *Silk Garden #234*
200 (200, 250)g *Cash Iroha #7*

Needles
One pair size 9 (5.5mm) straight needles
or size to obtain gauge
One 30"/80cm size 7 (4.5mm) circular needle
or size to obtain gauge

Gauge
17 sts/23 rows = 4"/10cm in St st with
Silk Garden or *Cash Iroha*
Take time to check gauge.

RIB PATTERN
Row 1 (RS) Knit.
Row 2 (WS) K1, *p5, k7, rep from *,
end with p5, k1.
Repeat these 2 rows throughout.

野呂

Hedvig Rollneck Sweater continued

BACK

With *Cash Iroha,* cast on 91 (103, 115) sts and work in Rib St patt starting with Row 1 until piece measures 4¾"/12cm (all sizes), ending with a WS row. Change to *Silk Garden* and knit 2 rows. Continue in St st until piece measures 14 (14½, 15)"/35.5 (37, 38)cm for short version or 19½ (20, 20½)"/49.5 (51, 52)cm for long version. Bind off all sts across next row.

FRONT

Cast on and work as for Back.

Join shoulder seams leaving a 14"/35.5 cm opening for neck (all sizes).

SLEEVES

From RS and with *Cash Iroha,* pick up 77 (81, 85) sts along *Silk Garden* armhole edge.

Next row (WS) K6 (8, 10) sts, * p5, k7, rep from *, end with p5, k6 (8, 10) sts.

Next row (RS) Knit.

Repeat these 2 rows until Sleeve measures 5"/12.5cm (all sizes).

Bind off all sts across next row.

FINISHING

With WS facing and circular needle, pick up 96 sts around neck opening (all sizes).

Next row (RS) *K7, p5, rep from * around neck opening.

Next row (WS) Knit.

Repeat these 2 rows for 3¼"/8cm or desired length (all sizes).

Join sleeve and side seams. ■

野呂 43

Cuernavaca Collared Tank

This A-line top is knit in *Cash Iroha* and with a collar and bottom edge worked in *Silk Garden*. Short-row shaping gives the collar its rounded shape. Knit here in brights, it could easily be calmed down with more neutral colors.

Sizes
S (S2, M, M2, L)

Finished Measurements
▓ Bust 33 (34½, 36, 38, 40)"/84 (88, 92, 96, 100)cm
▓ Length 25½ (26½, 27, 27½, 28)"/65 (67, 69, 70, 71)cm

Yarn
200 (250, 250, 300, 300)g *Cash Iroha* #111
150 (150, 150, 150, 150)g *Silk Garden* #87

Needles
One pair each size 8 (5 mm) and 9 (6 mm) straight needles *or size to obtain gauge*

Gauges
16 sts/22 rows = 4"/10cm in St st with *Cash Iroha* and size 9 (6mm) needles
18 sts/24 rows = 4"/10cm in St st with *Silk Garden* and size 8 (5mm) needles
Take time to check gauge.

NOTE
All decs are worked inside the 2 outermost sts at each side.

HORIZONTAL STRIPE PATTERN
Row 1 (RS) Knit.
Row 2 (WS) Purl.
Row 3 Knit.
Row 4 Purl.
Row 5 Purl.
Row 6 Knit.
Rep these 6 rows.

野呂

45

Cuernavaca Collared Tank

CURVED HORIZONTAL STRIPE PATTERN

Row 1 (RS) K6, sl 1 with yarn in front, turn work, sl 1 wyf, p6.

Row 2 (RS) K12, sl 1 wyf, turn work, sl 1 wyf, p12.

Row 3 (RS) Knit.

Row 4 (WS) Purl.

Row 5 (RS) Purl.

Row 6 (WS) Knit.

Rep these 6 rows.

BACK

With size 9 (6mm) needles and *Cash Iroha*, cast on 98 (100, 102, 106, 110) sts and work in St st. Dec 1 st at each side of every 6 rows, 15 times (all sizes)—68 (70, 72, 76, 80) sts.

▨ Armhole

When piece measures 16½ (17¼, 18, 18¾, 19½)"/42 (44, 46, 48, 49.5)cm, bind off 5 sts at beg of next 2 rows (all sizes). Thereafter bind off 2 sts at beg of next 10 rows (all sizes). Bind off rem sts over next RS row in knit.

FRONT
Work as for Back.

COLLAR (all sizes; make 2)
With size 5 (8mm) needles and *Silk Garden*, cast on 18 sts. Work in Horizontal Stripe pattern starting with Row 1. Rep 10 times. Change to Curved Horizontal Stripe pattern and rep 18 times. Change to Horizontal Stripe pattern and rep 10 times. Bind off.

BORDER EDGING
With size 5 (8mm) needles and *Silk Garden*, cast on 6 sts. Work in Horizontal Stripe Pattern until piece measures 49 (50, 51, 53, 55)"/124.5 (127, 129.5, 134.5, 140)cm. Leave open sts on a holder in case you need to adjust the length.

FINISHING
Join side seams.

▦ Border edging
Pin border to bottom edge of body so that the border covers the cast-on edge. Check border length, adding or subtracting rows as necessary. Bind off. Join border to body piece along the uppermost edge of the border.

▦ Collar
Place collar pieces with WS together and join. Fold collar along seams with RS out. The seams are at the shoulder. Pin collar to front and back of body approx 7"/18cm from shoulder seam, leaving approx 6½–7"/16–18cm at center front. Try on for fit and adjust as necessary. Join collar to top of body with invisible sts. The bottom hangs loosely over the body. ■

Using multicolored yarns with solid-colored ones in the same garment can enhance the beauty of both.

Victoria Cabled Pullover

I must admit I actually designed this sweater for myself! I am a real fan of *Kochoran* and love the way the simple cables create just enough texture to show off the yarn to its full advantage.

Sizes
S (M, L)

Finished Measurements
▦ Bust 34 (38, 42)"/86 (96.5, 107)cm
▦ Length 19 (20, 21)"/48 (51, 53)cm

Yarn
400 (500, 500)g *Kochoran* #55

Needles
One pair size 11 (8mm) straight needles
or size to obtain gauge

Gauge
13 sts = 4"/10cm in St st
Take time to check gauge.

STITCH GLOSSARY
FC cable Sl next 2 sts onto cable needle and leave at front of work, k2, k2 sts from cable needle.

CABLE PATTERN
Rows 1, 3 and 5 P3, * k4, p4, rep from *, end with k4, p3.
Rows 2 and 4 K3, * p4, k4, rep from *, end with p4, k3.
Row 6 P3, * FC cable, p4, rep from *, end with p3.
Repeat these 6 rows throughout.

BACK
Cast on 66 (74, 82) sts and work cable pattern from Row 1 until piece measures 12¾"/30cm.

▦ Armhole
Bind off 7 sts at beg of next 2 rows (all sizes). Work evenly until armhole measures 7 (8, 9)"/18 (20, 23)cm.

Neck (RS)

Bind off 10 (14, 18) sts, work to end.

Next row (WS) Bind off 10 (14, 18) sts.
Place rem 32 (32, 32) sts on a stitch holder.

FRONT

Cast on and work as for Back.

SLEEVES

Cast on 34 (34, 42) sts and work in
Cable pattern from Row 1.

Size Small

Inc 1 st at each side every 6 rows
14 times—62 sts.

Size Medium

Inc 1 st at each side every 6 rows,
10 times and every 4 rows 8 times—70 sts.

Size Large

Inc 1 st at each side every 6 rows,
10 times and every 4 rows 7 times—76 sts.
Incorporate the incs into the cable pattern.
Work until piece measures 19¾ (20¼,
20¾)"/50 (51.5, 53)cm. At beg of next
2 rows, bind off 7 sts once and 2 sts 3 times
(all sizes). Bind off rem sts.

FINISHING

Join right shoulder seam. Transfer all neck sts
onto one needle. Inc 1 st at beg of row and
1 st at end of row. (These are selvage sts
and will disappear in the collar seam).
Continue in Cable patt as established. Work
8 rows. Bind off all sts loosely. Join collar
seams and left shoulder seam. Join sleeves and
fit into armholes. Join sleeves to armholes. Join
side seams. ■

Horndal Hat and Scarf

The alternation of *Blossom* in garter stitch and *Kureyon* in rib stitch creates the feeling of both horizontal and vertical striping in the scarf. The little cup at the top of the hat lends a touch of whimsy.

Size
Adult

Finished Measurements
■ Hat circumference approx 22"/56cm
■ Scarf width 6¾"/17cm
■ Scarf length 75""/186cm

Yarn
■ Hat
Approx 50g *Kureyon* #154
Approx 50g *Blossom* #5
■ Scarf
Approx 100g *Kureyon* #154
Approx 100g *Blossom* #5

Needles
One pair size 9 (5.5mm) straight needles
or size to obtain gauge

Gauges
15 sts/30 rows = 4"/10 cm in Gst with *Kureyon*
Approx 12 sts/17 rows = 4"/10 cm in Rib st with *Blossom*
Take time to check gauge.

NOTES
■ The hat is knit flat and seamed at the back.
■ If you have trouble locating *Blossom*, this pattern can be knit in *Kochoran* using the same amount of yarn and size needles.

RIB STITCH
Row 1 (RS) K2, *p2, k2, rep from*.
Row 2 (WS) P2, *k2, p2, rep from*.
Rep these 2 rows.

HAT
Cast on 84 sts with *Kureyon* and work 5½"/14 cm in Gst, ending with a WS row.

■ **Blossom Section**
Next row (RS) With *Blossom* and working in Rib st, dec 8 sts evenly across row—76 sts.
Continue with *Blossom* in Rib st for 3"/7.5 cm, ending with a WS row.

Kureyon Section

First dec row (RS) With *Kureyon,* knit 2 tog across row—38 sts.

Knit 3 rows evenly.

Second dec row (RS) Knit the 5th and 6th sts tog across row—32 sts.

Knit 3 rows evenly.

Third dec row (RS) Knit the 4th and 5th sts tog across row—26 sts.

Knit 1 row.

Fourth dec row (RS) Knit 2 tog across row—13 sts.

Knit 1 row.

Fifth dec row (RS) Knit 2 tog across row, end with k1—7 sts.

Knit 4 rows evenly.

Next row (RS) Inc 6 sts evenly across row—13 sts.

Knit 3 rows.

Next row (RS) Knit, inc 3 sts evenly across row—16 sts.

Knit 1 row.

Change to *Blossom* and knit 1 row.

Bind off all sts in *Blossom* over next row.

SCARF

Cast on 26 sts with *Kureyon* and work 4"/10cm in Gst, ending with a WS row.

Blossom Section

Next row (RS) With *Blossom,* work in Rib st, dec 4 sts evenly across row—22 sts.

Continue with *Blossom* in Rib st for 7"/18 cm ending with a WS row.

Kureyon Section

Next row (RS) With *Kureyon,* knit, inc 4 sts evenly across row—26 sts. Continue with *Kureyon* in Gst for 8"/20.5 cm. Rep these 2 sections 3 more times.

Rep *Blossom* section one more time.

Next row (RS) With *Kureyon,* knit, inc 4 sts evenly across row—26 sts.

Continue with *Kureyon* in Gst for 4"/10cm. Bind off all sts. ■

Dorotea Pullover

This textured sweater is another development of my elongated buttonhole theme (see Ekeby Vest on page 34). This time *Silk Mountain* forms the hole rows against a background of *Kureyon*. Since both yarns are worked at the same gauge, the *Kureyon* is looser than you would normally expect to find, lending drape to the fabric.

SIZES
S (M, L)

Finished Measurements
▥ Bust 34 (38½, 42½)"/86 (98, 108)cm
▥ Length 22 (24, 26)"/56 (61, 66)cm

Yarn
450 (500, 550)g *Silk Mountain* #6
200 (200, 200)g *Kureyon* #183

Needles
One pair size 10 (6mm) straight needles
or size to obtain gauge
One size I/9 (5.5mm) or J/10 (6mm) crochet hook

Gauge
14 sts = 4"/10cm with *Kureyon* and *Silk Mountain* in St st
Take time to check gauge.

NOTE
If you have trouble locating *Silk Mountain*, this pattern can be knit in *Iro* or *Furisode* using the same amount of yarn and size needles.

HOLE STRIPE PATTERN
▥ Hole Stripe A
Row 1 and 3 (RS) With *Kureyon*, knit.
Row 2 and 4 (WS) Purl.
Row 5 (RS) With *Silk Mountain*, knit.
Row 6 (WS) With *Silk Mountain*, k4, *bind off 4 sts, k4, rep from*.
Row 7 (RS) With *Silk Mountain*, k4, *cast on 4 sts, k4, rep from*.
Row 8 (WS) With *Silk Mountain*, knit.

▥ Hole Stripe B
Row 9 and 11 (RS) With *Kureyon*, knit.
Row 10 and 12 (WS) With *Kureyon*, purl.
Row 13 With *Silk Mountain*, knit.
Row 14 With *Silk Mountain*, k8, *bind off 4

sts, k4, rep from*, end with k4.

Row 15 (RS) With *Silk Mountain*, k8, *cast on 4 sts, k4, rep from*, end with k4.

Row 16 With *Silk Mountain*, knit.

Repeat Rows 1–16 throughout.

BODY

▦ Lower Front

With *Kureyon*, cast on 60 (68, 76) sts and work in Hole Stripe patt starting with Row 1. Repeat Hole Stripe patterns ABABA (ABABAB, ABABAB). Piece now measures approx 8 (10, 10)"/20 (25.5, 25.5)cm.

▦ Front sleeve shaping

Work Row 9 (1, 1), casting on 36 (36, 36) sts at end of the row. Turn and work back, casting on 36 (36, 36) sts at end of row. Continue to work in Hole Stripe pattern over all 132 (140, 148) sts. Repeat Hole Stripe patterns BAB (ABA, ABAB). Then work Rows 1–4 (9–12, 1–4).

Neck opening
Next row Working Row 5 (13, 5), work 56 (60, 64) sts. Bind off 20 sts (all sizes). Work 56 (60, 64) sts to end. Work each side of neck opening separately. Continue to work in Hole Stripe pattern as established ABA plus rows 1–3 (BAB plus rows 9–11, ABA plus rows 1–3).

Next row (WS) With *Silk Mountain*, work 56 (60, 64) sts, cast on 20 sts (all sizes), work 56 (60, 64) sts to end. Continue to work in Hole Stripe pattern as established over all 132 (140, 148) sts. Repeat Hole Stripe pattern BABA (ABAB, BABAB). Work Row 9 (1, 1).

Back sleeve shaping
Bind off 36 sts at beg of next 2 rows (all sizes)—60 (68, 76) sts.

Lower Back
Continue in Hole Stripe pattern as established BABAB (ABABAB, ABABAB). Work Rows 1–4 (1–4, 1–4). Bind off.

BODY EDGINGS
With *Silk Mountain*, pick up 63 (68, 73) sts at bottom of Front Body. Knit 2 rows.

Row 1 (WS) K2, *p4, k1, repeat from *, end with p4, k2.

Row 2 P2, *k4, p1, repeat from *, end with k4, p2.

Work rows 1 and 2 for 1½"/ 4cm (all sizes).

Row 3 (WS) K2, *p4, m1, k1, m1, repeat from *, end with p4, k2.

Row 4 P2, *k4, p3, repeat from *, end with k4, p2.

Repeat Rows 3 and 4 until edging measures 5"/13cm or desired length.

Bind off all sts in rib over next row.

Work same as above for Back Body.

SLEEVE EDGING
With *Silk Mountain*, pick up 43 (48, 53) sts at bottom of Sleeve. Knit 2 rows.

Work in rib pattern same as for Body Edging.

FINISHING
Join side and sleeve seams. Work 1 row of single crochet around neck opening. ■

Antoinette Vest

This roomy vest features a racer-back shoulder, which gives it a casual look. Knit in seed stitch with *Iro*, it can also be worked in *Silk Garden Chunky*. The look can easily be changed by adding to the length as desired before the armhole shaping.

Sizes
XS (S, M, L)

Finished Measurements
▓ Chest 34 (38, 42, 46)"/86 (96.5, 106.5, 117)cm
▓ Length 21 (21¾, 22¼, 23)"/53.5 (55, 56.5, 58)cm

Yarn
300 (300, 400, 400)g *Iro #78*

Needles
One pair size 11 (8mm) straight needles *or size to obtain gauge*

Gauge
12 sts/20 rows = 4"/10cm in Seed st
Take time to check gauge.

NOTES
▓ The edges of this garment are self-finishing. For a smoother edge, add a row of single crochet.
▓ There is no Back armhole measurement, as it does not correspond to the Front armhole; the bind-off edge curves up to meet the straps of the Front.

BACK
Cast on 52 (58, 64, 70) sts and work in Seed st for 11"/28 cm (all sizes).

Antoinette Vest continued

▓ Armhole

Bind off 4 (4, 5, 5) sts at each side once, then 2 sts 5 (6, 7, 8) times and 1 st 3 (3,3, 3) times—18 (20, 20, 22) sts. Work evenly for 6 rows. Inc 2 sts at each side 5 (6, 7, 8) times and thereafter 1 st 3 (3, 3, 3) times—44 (50, 54, 60) sts. Bind off all sts across next row.

FRONT

Cast on and work as for Back until piece measures 11"/28 cm.

▓ Armhole

Bind off 4 (4, 6, 6) sts at each side once, then 2 sts 1 (2, 2, 3) times and 1 st once (all sizes)—38 (40, 42, 44) sts.
Work evenly until piece measures 13 (13½, 14, 14½)"/33 (34.5, 35.5, 36.5)cm.

▓ Neck Opening

Bind off middle 10 (10, 12, 12) sts, work to end. Work each side of neck opening separately.

Work back to neck opening, and bind off from neck edge 2 sts once and 1 st 3 times (all sizes)—9 (10, 10, 11) sts. Work evenly until armhole measures 10 (10¾, 11¼, 11¾)"/ 25.5 (27, 28.5, 30)cm. Bind off all sts over next row. Work other side of neck opening identically but reverse the shaping.

FINISHING

Join cast-off edge of Front shoulder straps to cast-off sts of Back. Join side seams. ▪

Self-finishing edges are a fun design element to experiment with, especially when an edging would complicate things visually by introducing more colors or textures.

Bettna Long Cardigan

This cardigan is similar in construction to the Klaralund Kimono Sweater (see page 31). Stitches are added at the armhole to lower the horizontal seam across the body and give the garment a more relaxed fit. You can easily change the length by shortening or lengthening the bottom piece.

Sizes
XS (S, S2, M, M2, L, XL)

Finished Measurements
▨ Bust 34 (36, 38, 40, 42, 44, 46)"/86 (91.5, 96.5, 101.5, 107, 112, 117)cm
▨ Length 28 (28¼, 28¾, 28¾, 29¼, 29¼, 30)"/71 (72, 73, 73, 74.5, 74.5, 76)cm

Yarn
500 (550, 600, 650, 650, 700, 750)g
Silk Garden #211

Needles
One pair size 8 (5mm) straight needles
or size to obtain gauge.

Gauge
16 sts/22 rows = 4"/10 cm in St st
16 sts/32 rows = 4"/10 cm in Gst
Take time to check gauge.

EXTENDED GARTER STITCH
Row 1 Knit.
Row 2 Purl.
Rows 3 and 4 Knit.
Repeat these 4 rows.

LOWER BACK
Cast on 68 (72, 76, 80, 84, 88, 92) sts and knit 14 rows.
Next row (RS): Change to St st, beg with a k row. Work evenly until piece measures 15½ (16, 16½, 16½, 17, 17, 17½)"/39.5 (40.5, 42, 42, 43, 43, 44.5)cm. Bind off all sts.

LOWER RIGHT FRONT
Cast on 34 (36, 38, 40, 42, 44, 46) sts and knit 14 rows.
Next row (RS) Change to St st, beg with a k row. Work evenly until piece measures 15½ (16, 16½, 16½, 17, 17, 17½)"/39.5 (40.5, 42, 42, 43, 43, 44.5)cm. Bind off all sts.

Bettna Long Cardigan continued

LOWER LEFT FRONT
Cast on and work as for Lower Right Front.

SLEEVE AND RIGHT UPPER BODY
Cast on 58 (58, 60, 62, 62, 64, 64) sts and knit 14 rows (all sizes).

Next row (RS) Change to St st, beg with a k row. Inc 1 st at each side when piece measures 6"/1 cm and then again when piece measures 10"/25cm. Work evenly until piece measures 16½ (16½, 16½, 16, 16, 15½, 15½)"/42 (42, 42, 40.5, 40.5, 39.5, 39.5)cm ending with a RS row.

Next row (WS) Knit 7 rows, casting on 20 sts at end of last row (all sizes). Change to Extended Gst. Work Row 1, casting on 20 sts at end of row (all sizes). Cont working in Extended Gst until piece measures 8½ (9, 9½, 10, 10½, 11, 11½)"/21.5 (23, 24, 25.5, 26.5, 28, 29)cm, ending with Row 1.

Next row (WS) Bind off 38 sts (all sizes), work Row 2 to end. Place rem sts on a holder.

SLEEVE AND LEFT UPPER BODY
Cast on and work as for Sleeve and Right Upper Body until piece measures 8½ (9, 9½, 10, 10½, 11, 11½)"/21.5 (23, 24, 25.5, 26.5, 28, 29)cm, ending with Row 2.

Next row (RS) Bind off 38 sts (all sizes), work Row 3 to end. Place rem sts on a holder.

FINISHING
▦ Right Front Edging and Back Neck
Match bind-off edge of Lower Right Front to the right-side edge of Upper Right Front and join. Pick up 62 (64, 66, 66, 68, 68, 70) sts evenly spaced along right edge of Lower Right Front and knit up all the open sts of Upper Right Front.

(All sizes) Next row (WS) Bind off 2 sts, knit to end.

Next row (RS) Knit.

Next row (WS) Bind off 1 st, knit to end.

Next row Knit. Repeat last 2 rows 4 more times. Knit 1 row.

Next row (WS) Bind off all sts.

▦ Left Front Edging and Back Neck
Match bind-off edge of Lower Left Front to the left-side edge of Upper Left Front and join. Knit the open sts from holder and then pick up 62 (64, 66, 66, 68, 68, 70) sts evenly spaced along left-side edge of Lower Left Front.

(All sizes) Next row (WS) Knit.

Next row (RS) Bind off 2 sts, knit to end.

Next row Knit.

Next row (RS) Bind off 1 st, knit to end.

Next row Knit. Repeat last 2 rows 4 more times.

Next row (WS) Bind off all sts.

Join edging at back neck. Join sleeve and side seams. ▪

Viggeby Dog Coat

For the pooch who wants to look his or her Sunday best! This luxurious dog coat with decorative buttons is secured with a strap that goes around the belly. It is easy to put on and easy to size; just follow the guidelines below.

Size
Small dog (e.g., Jack Russell, miniature poodle; for other sizes see note below)

Finished Measurements
▥ Width approx 16"/40.5cm
▥ Length approx 12"/30.5cm

Yarn
100g *Iro* #9

Needles
One pair size 10½ (7mm) straight needles *or size to obtain gauge*

Extras
4 3/4"/2cm buttons

Gauge
12 sts/16 rows = 4"/10cm in St st
Take time to check gauge.

NOTES
▥ This coat is based on two measurements. The first is from elbow to elbow over the shoulders (in this case 16"/40.5cm). The second is length of back from middle of shoulder blades to base of tail (in this case 12"/30.5cm). Find these two measurements for your dog. Adjusting this pattern is easy: When casting on, add or subtract 3 sts for every 1"/2.5cm difference in the elbow-to-elbow measurement. The length is easy to regulate by fitting the dog during the knitting. The strap should be checked for length before binding off.

▥ This pattern can also be knit in *Silk Garden Chunky* using the same amount of yarn and size needles.

COAT
Cast on 53 sts.
Rows 1, 3 and 5 (WS) K1, p1, k24, p1, k24, p1, k1.

野呂 67

All RS rows K1, sl 1, k2tog, k22, m1, sl 1, make 1, k22, k2tog, sl 1, k1.

Rows 7, 9 and 11 (WS) Purl.

Rows 13 and 15 (WS) K1, p1, k24, p1, k24, p1, k1.

Repeat Rows 6–15 throughout.

Work evenly until piece measures approximately 14"/35.5cm, ending with Row 15. Knit 2 rows. Bind off all sts.

STRAP

With RS facing and starting 2"/5cm from back bind-off, pick up 9 sts along right side edge. Work in Garter st for 6½"/16.5cm or to desired length. Bind off. Sew 2 buttons side by side near end of strap after checking for fit.

FINISHING

Place markers on body corresponding to buttons on strap. Work 1 row of single crochet around all edges to stabilize, working 2 buttonholes at markers as follows: Chain 2 sts, skip 2 rows along knit edge, work 3 sc along knit edge, chain 2 sts, skip 2 rows along knit edge.

Place coat in position on dog, cross the front points in front of chest snugly. Pin. Remove coat over the dog's head. Sew together front points as pinned along overlapping edges using backstitch. Sew on 2 buttons corresponding to the front points for double-breasted effect. ∎

Lövlund Zigzag Sweater

The graceful shape of this top is formed by the placement of the double increases and decreases. It is worked in two pieces with the sleeves being cast onto the body at the armholes. For longer sleeves, simply cast on more stitches!

Sizes
S (M, L, XL)

Finished Measurements
- Bust 33 (36¼, 39½, 42½)"/84 (92, 100, 108)cm
- Length 20 (20½, 21, 21½)"/51 (52, 53, 54)cm

Yarn
160 (200, 240, 280)g *Hanna Silk* #33

Needles
One pair size 8 (5mm) straight needles *or size to obtain gauge*

Gauge
16 sts /20 rows = 4"/10cm in St st
Take time to check gauge.

NOTE
If you have trouble locating *Hanna Silk*, this pattern can be knit in *Silk Garden* or *Taiyo* using the same amount of yarn and size needles.

.
BACK
Cast on *77 (83, 89, 95)* sts.
Row 1 (RS) P1, p2tog, p14 (16, 18, 20), m1, sl 1 p-wise, m1, p18 (19, 20, 21), p2tog, sl 1 p-wise, p2tog, p18 (19, 20, 21), m1, sl 1 p-wise, m1, p14 (16, 18, 20), p2tog, p1.
Row 2 (WS) K17 (19, 21, 23), p1, k20 (21, 22, 23), p1, k20 (21, 22, 23), p1, k17 (19, 21, 23).
Rep these 2 rows until piece measures 13"/33cm *at side edge* (all sizes).

▦ Armhole (RS)
Cast on 18 (19, 19, 20) sts at end of next 2 rows for sleeves—113 (121, 127, 135) sts.

Next Row (RS) P1, p2tog, p33 (35, 37, 39), m1, sl 1 p-wise, m1, p18 (19, 20, 21), p2tog, sl 1 p-wise, p2tog, p18 (19, 20, 21), m1, sl 1 p-wise, m1, p33 (35, 37, 39), p2tog, p1.

Next Row (WS) K36 (38, 40, 42), p1, k20 (21, 22, 23), p1, k20 (21, 22, 23), p1, k36 (38, 40, 42). Cont working over all sts until piece measures 7¼ (8, 8½, 9)"/19 (20, 21¼, 23)cm from cast-on row of sleeve. Bind off all sts over next WS row.

FRONT
Cast on and work as for back until piece measures 13"/33cm (all sizes).

▧ Armhole
Cast on sleeve sts as for back and work over all sts until piece measures 13½"/34cm (all sizes).

FRONT NECK
Next row (RS) Work 41 (44, 46, 49) sts as established. Bind off middle 31 (33, 35, 37) sts. Work to end of row and back to neck opening. Work each side of neck opening separately.

Next row (RS) P1, p2tog, p2, m1, sl 1 p-wise, m1, purl to end.

Next row (WS) Work as established above, ending row with k5. Rep the last 2 rows until piece measures 7½ (8, 8½, 9)"/19 (20, 21.5, 23)cm from cast-on row of sleeve. Bind off all sts over next WS row. Work other side of neck opening in the same way, reversing the shaping.

FINISHING
Join shoulder seams. Join sleeve and side seams. Steam-block shoulder seams lightly under a damp dishtowel to flatten if desired. ▰

Sursa Ruffled Shawl

This simple shawl is worked from end to end using a double strand of *Silk Garden* with a slightly larger needle than you would use for most sweaters. It is then edged with a doubled *Cash Iroha* ruffle that weighs down the short sides and highlights the drape of the *Silk Garden*. The respective yarns are worked double-stranded throughout. The shawl shown here is knitted using both ends of one skein of yarn simultaneously.

Size
Adult

Finished Measurements
■ Width approx 23"/5 cm
■ Length Approx 75"/190cm

Yarn
Approx 250g *Silk Garden* #87
Approx 100g *Cash Iroha* #77

Needles
One 30"/80cm size 15 (10mm) circular needle *or size to obtain gauge*

Gauge
Approx 10 sts/12 rows = 4"/10cm in St st with *Silk Garden* held double
Take time to check gauge

NOTE
All selvage sts are knitted on RS and purled on WS rows.

SHAWL
Cast on 3 sts in *Silk Garden* held double.
Inc row 1 (RS) K1, 1 yo, k to end of row.
Row 2 (WS) Purl, purling yo from previous row.
Rep rows 1 and 2 until almost halfway through the third skein of yarn (approx 125g), ending with a WS row.
Dec row 1 (RS) K1, yo, k2tog, k to end.
Dec row 2 (WS) Purl to last 4 sts, p2tog, p1 in yo from previous row, p1.
Repeat these last 2 rows until 3 sts remain.
Pull yarn end through rem sts to fasten off.

RUFFLE
From RS of work and using *Cash Iroha* held double, pick up 1 st for every row along the two short sides of shawl starting at one end. For best result, pick up each st in middle of edge st leaving the yo untouched.
Next row (WS) K1, * make 1, k1, rep from * to end.
Next row (RS) Purl. Work 5 more rows in reverse St st.
Bind off all sts over next row. ■

野呂

Julita Tunic

This lovely tunic is worked from the bottom up and features four-stitch cables that move together and then integrate to form points, creating a flattering A-line shape. This pattern is for the experienced knitter.

Sizes
S (M, L)

Finished Measurements
- Bust 33 (36, 39)"/84 (91.5, 99)cm
- Length 28 (28½, 29)"/71 (72.5, 74)cm
- Sleeve length 18½ (18½, 19)"/47 (47, 48)cm

Yarn
500 (550, 600)g *Cash Iroha* in #1

Needles
One pair size 7 (4.5mm) straight needles *or size to obtain gauge*

Extras
Cable needle

Gauge
16 sts/24rows = 4"/10cm square in reverse St st
Take time to check gauge.

STITCH GLOSSARY
C4F Sl next 2 sts onto cable needle and hold at front of work, k2, k2 sts from cable needle.
C4B Sl next 2 sts onto cable needle and hold at back of work, k2, k2 sts from cable needle.

BACK
Cast on 110 (115, 120) sts.
Row 1, 3 and 5 K12 (14, 16), (p4, k7) 3 times, p4, k12 (13, 14), (p4, k7) 3 times, p4, k12 (14, 16).
Row 2 P12 (14, 16), (k4, p7) 3 times, k4, p12 (13, 14), (k4, p7) 3 times, k4, p12 (14, 16).
Row 4 P12 (14, 16), C4F, k7, C4F, p7, C4B, p7, C4B, k12 (13, 14) C4F, k7, C4F, k7, C4B, p7, C4B, p12 (14, 16).

Julita Tunic

Row 6 Same as Row 2.

These 6 rows make up the basic cable pattern.

When piece measures 2"/5cm, work dec row as follows:

First dec row (RS) P12 (14, 16), (k4, p2tog, p5) 3 times, k4, m1, p12 (13, 14), m1, (k4, p5, p2tog) 3 times, k4, p12 (14, 16)—106 (111, 116) sts.

When piece measures 4"/10cm, work dec row as follows:

Second dec row (RS) P12 (14, 16), (k4, p2tog, p4) 3 times, k4, m1, p14 (15, 16), m1, (k4, p4, p2tog) 3 times, k4, p12 (14, 16)—102 (107, 112) sts.

When piece measures 6"/15cm, work dec row as follows:

Third dec row (RS) P12 (14, 16), (k4, p2tog, p3) 3 times, k4, p16 (17, 18), (k4, p3, p2tog) 3 times, k4, p12 (14, 16)—96 (101, 106) sts.

When piece measures 8"/20cm, work dec row as follows:

Fourth dec row (RS) P12 (14, 16), (k4, p2tog, p2) 3 times, k4, p16 (17, 18), (k4, p2, p2tog) 3 times, k4, p12 (14, 16)—90 (95, 100) sts.

When piece measures 10"/25.5cm, work dec row as follows:

Fifth dec row (RS) P12 (14, 16), (k4, p2tog, p1) 3 times, k4, p16 (17, 18), (k4, p1, p2tog) 3 times, k4, p12 (14, 16)—84 (89, 94) sts.
***

Next row (WS) K12 (14, 16), m1, (p4, k2) 3 times, p4, m1, k16 (17, 18), m1, (p4, k2) 3 times, p4, m1, k12 (14, 16)—88 (93, 98) sts.

When piece measures 12"/30.5cm, work dec row as follows:

Sixth dec row (RS) P13 (15, 17), (k4, p2tog) 3 times, k4, p18 (19, 20), (k4, p2tog) 3 times, k4, p13 (15, 17)—82 (87, 93) sts.

Next row (WS) K13 (15, 17), m1, (p4, k2) 3 times, p4, m1, k18 (19, 20), m1, (p4, k2) 3 times, p4, m1, K13 (15, 17)—86 (91, 97) sts.

When piece measures approx 14"/35.5cm and ending with row 5 of cable patt, work dec row as follows:

Final dec row (WS) K14 (16, 18), (p3, p2tog) 3 times, p4, k20 (21, 22), (p3, p2tog) 3 times, p4, k14 (16, 18)—80 (84, 88) sts.

Next row (RS) P14 (16, 18), k16, p20 (21, 22), k16, p14 (16, 18).

Next row (WS) Work sts as presented.

Row 3 P18 (20, 22) *k2, sl 1, k1, psso, k2tog, k2*, p28 (29, 30), rep between * *, p18 (20, 22).

Row 5 P18 (20, 22), *k1, sl 1, k1, psso, k2tog, k1*, p28 (29, 30), rep between * *, p18 (20, 22).

Row 7 P18 (20, 22), *sl 1, k1, psso, k2tog*, p28 (29, 30), rep between * *, p18 (20, 22).

Row 8 (WS) K18 (20, 22), p2tog, p28 (29, 30), p2tog, k18 (20, 22)—66 (71, 77) sts. Work evenly in reverse St st until piece measures 20"/51cm (all sizes).

▦ Armhole

Bind off 4 sts at beg of next 2 rows. Thereafter bind off at each side every other row, 2 sts once and 1 st twice for armholes. When piece measures 28 (28½, 29)"/71 (72.5, 74)cm, bind off 9 (11, 13) sts at beg of next 2 rows. Place sts rem 32 (33, 35) on stitch holder.

FRONT

Cast on and work as for back until ***.

When piece measures 12"/30.5cm, work dec row as follows:

Sixth dec row (RS) P12 (14, 16), (k4, p2tog) 3 times, k4, p16 (17, 18), (k4, p2tog) 3 times, k4, p12 (14, 16)—78 (83, 88) sts.

▦ Point of Cable

Row 1 (RS) P14 (16, 18), *sl next 4 sts to cable needle and hold at front of work, p4, k4 sts from cable needle, sl next 4 sts to cable needle and hold at back of work, k4, p4 sts from cable needle*, p20 (21, 22), rep between * *, end with p14 (16, 18).

Rows 2, 4 and 6 Work sts as they are presented.

Julita Tunic continued

When piece measures approx 14"/35.5cm and ending with row 5 of cable pattern, work dec row as follows:

Final dec row (WS) K12 (14, 16), (p3, p2tog) 3 times, p4, k16 (17, 18), (p3, p2tog) 3 times, p4, k12 (14, 16)—72 (77, 82) sts.

Next row (RS) P12 (14, 16), k16, p16(17,18), k16, p12 (14, 16).

Next row (WS) Work sts as presented.

▓ Point of Cable

Row 1 (RS) P12 (14, 16), *sl next 4 sts to cable needle and hold at front of work, p4, k4 sts from cable needle, sl next 4 sts to cable needle and hold at back of work, k4, p4 sts from cable needle*, p18 (19, 20), rep between * *, end with p12 (14, 16).

Row 2 (WS) K16 (18, 20), m1, p8, m1, k24 (25, 26), m1, p8, m1, k16 (18, 20).

Row 3 P17 (19, 21), * k2, sl 1, k1, psso, k2tog, k2, p26 (27, 28)*, rep between * *, p17 (19, 21).

Row 4 K17 (19, 21), m1, p6, m1, k26 (27, 28), m1, p6, m1, k17 (19, 21).

Row 5 P18 (20, 22), * k1, sl 1, k1, psso, k2tog, k1, p28 (29, 30)*, rep between * *, p18 (20, 22).

Row 6 K18 (20, 22), m1, p4, m1, k28 (29, 30), m1, p6, m1, k18 (20, 22).

Row 7 P19 (21, 23), * sl 1, k1, psso, k2tog, p30 (31, 32)*, rep between * *, p19 (21, 23).

Row 8 K19 (21, 23), p2tog, k16 (17, 18), p2tog, k30 (31, 32)—70 (75, 80) sts. Work evenly in Reverse St st until piece measures 20"/51cm (all sizes).

▓ Armhole

Bind off 4 sts at beg of next 2 rows. Thereafter bind off at each side every other row, 2 sts once and 1 st 4 times for armholes. Work evenly until piece measures 26 (26½, 27)"/66 (67, 68.5)cm ending with a WS row.

▓ Front Neck

(RS) Work each side of neck separately. P17 (19, 21) sts. Turn and bind off 2 sts from left neck edge. Thereafter bind off from neck edge every other row, 2 sts once, and 1 st 4 times (all sizes). Work evenly until piece measures 28 (28½, 29)"/71 (72.5, 74)cm. Bind off. Place middle 16 (17, 18) sts on a stitch holder. Beg on RS at neck edge, work other side of neck opening the same, reversing the shaping.

SLEEVES

Cast on 61 (65, 69) sts and establish cable pattern as follows:

Row 1 and 3 K12 (14, 16), (p4, k7) 3 times, p4, k12 (14, 16).

Row 2, 4 and 6 P12 (14, 16), (k4, p7) 3 times, k4, p12 (14, 16).

Row 5 P12 (14, 16), C4F, p7, C4F, p7, C4B, p7, C4B, p12 (14, 16).

These 6 rows make up the basic cable pattern.

▥ Sleeve shaping

Work decs between cables (3 decs every dec row) as for back and front every 2¾"/7.5cm 6 times. *At same time (WS):* When piece measures 7"/18cm, inc 1 st at each side as follows: Work until 1 st before first cable, m1, work cables, m1, work to end. Inc 1 st at each side as described every 6 rows 8 more times—59 (63, 67) sts

Final dec row (WS) Work to first cable, (p3, p2tog) 3 times, p4, work to end.

Next 2 rows Work sts as they are presented.

▥ Point of Cable

Row 1 (RS) P to cables, sl next 4 sts to cable needle and hold at front of work, p4, k4 sts from cable needle, sl next 4 sts to cable needle and hold at back of work, k4, p4 sts from cable needle, p to end.

Rows 2, 4 and 6 Work sts as they are presented.

Row 3 P to point, m1, k2, sl 1, k1, psso, k2tog, k2, m1, p to end.

Row 5 P to point, m1, k1, sl 1, k1, psso, k2tog, k1, m1, p to end.

Row 7 P to point, m1, sl 1, k1, psso, k2tog, m1, p to end.

Row 8 (WS) K to point, p2tog, k to end—55 (59, 63) sts.

When piece measures 18¼ (18¼, 18½)"/ 47 (47, 48)cm, bind off at each side 4 sts once, 2 sts once, 1 st 3 times, 2 sts twice, 3 sts twice. Work 1 row. Bind off rem sts.

FINISHING

Join right shoulder seam. With RS of front facing, pick up 82 (84, 86) sts evenly around neck opening as follows: 15 sts along left front neck, k20 (21, 22) sts from stitch holder, pick up 15 sts evenly along right side of front neck, k32 (33, 34) sts across back neck. Work 6 rows in reverse St st and bind off loosely. Join left shoulder and collar seam. Fit sleeves to armhole, gathering extra sts at top of sleeve for a slight puff. Join. Join sleeve and body seams. ▪

Grinda Hat and Scarf

This coordinating hat and scarf set is knit simply in garter stitch, with the addition of buttonholes in the scarf pattern. Although quite easy to knit, the scarf is not for the finishing faint of heart—you will have quite a few yarn ends to weave in!

Size
Adult

Finished Measurements
▥ Hat circumference approx 21"/53cm
▥ Scarf width approx 6¾"/17cm
▥ Scarf length approx 75"/190cm

Yarn
▥ Hat
100g *Iro* #21
▥ Scarf
200g *Iro* #21

Needles
▥ Hat
One pair size 10½ (7mm) straight needles
or size to obtain gauge
▥ Scarf
One pair size 11 (8mm) straight needles
or size to obtain gauge

Gauge
11sts = 4"/10cm in Gst with size 10½ (7mm) needles
Take time to check gauge.

HAT
Cast on 64 sts and work in Gst for 4½"/11cm.

Next row Dec 8 sts evenly across row by knitting tog every 7th and 8th st—56 sts.

Next row Knit.

Repeat these 2 rows 5 times, working decs with one fewer st between them for every dec row.

Next row Knit 2 tog across row—8 sts.
Work evenly for 7 rows.
Bind off all sts.

SCARF
Cast on 22 sts.
Rows 1–4 Knit.
Row 5 K3, bind off 6 sts, k4, bind off
6 sts, k3. (There will be 4 sts on needle
between the 2 bound-off areas).
Row 6 K3, cast on 6 sts, k4, cast on
6 sts, k3.
Rows 7–10 Knit.
Row 11 Bind off 4 sts, k4, bind off 6 sts,
k4, bind off 4 sts. Break yarn. (There will be
4 sts on needle between bound-off areas.)
Row 12 Cast on 4 sts, k4, cast on 6 sts,
k4, cast on 4 sts.
Repeat these 12 rows throughout.
Work until yarn runs out, binding off all sts
after row 9.

FINISHING
Join seam at back. ■

 To learn more about the characteristics of different yarns, try swatching
the Grinda stitch pattern using various yarns in your stash.

Mora Chevron Vest

This design is similar in construction to the Lövlund Zigzag Sweater (see page 69). I again started with a basic V pattern, only this time to give form to a vest. It suits many body types, and the diagonal striping is very slimming.

Sizes
S (M, L)

Finished Measurements
- Bust 29 (31, 33)"/74 (79, 84)cm
- Length 26 (26, 26½)"/66 (67, 68.5)cm

Yarn
Approx 300 (350, 350)g *Silk Garden* #228

Needles
One pair each size 7 and 8 (4.5 and 5mm) straight needles *or size to obtain gauge*

Gauge
18 sts/24 rows = 4"/10cm square with size 8 (5mm) needles in St st
Take time to check gauge.

NOTES
- Bust measurements are taken without stretching. The fabric stretches later over the body to produce a close fit. Vest fits chest sizes 32–34 (34–36, 36–38)"/81–86.5 (86.5–91.5, 91.5–96.5) cm.
- Gauge should be attained while working in St st. The actual Rib st of the garment will then pull the fabric together.
- All side shaping is worked at inside of 2 outermost sts.

BACK
With smaller needles, cast on 79 (85, 91) sts. Work in Gst stripe as follows:

Row 1 (RS) K1, sl 1 p-wise, m1, k35 (38, 41) sts, k2tog tbl, sl 1 p-wise, k2tog, k35 (38, 41) sts, m1, sl 1 p-wise, k1.

Row 2 P2, k37 (40, 43) sts, p1, k37 (40, 43) sts, p2.

Row 3 Work as for Row 1.

Row 4 Work as for Row 2. Change to larger needles.

Row 5 Work as for Row 1.

Row 6 Purl.

Mora Chevron Vest

Row 7 Work as for Row 1.

Row 8 Purl.

These 8 rows will be repeated throughout *on larger needles*.

Work until piece measures 2 (2, 2)"/5 (5, 5)cm at side edge, ending with a WS row.

Next row (RS) Dec 2 sts across row by simply omitting the m1 at beg and end of this pattern row. Repeat decs every 6 rows 3 more times— 71 (77, 83) sts. Work 4 rows according to pattern.

Next row (RS) Inc 2 sts at either side of the center st by omitting the decs on this pattern row. Rep incs every 8 rows 3 more times—79 (85, 91) sts. Work according to Garter stripe patt until piece measures 12¼ (12¼, 12½)"/31 (31, 32)cm.

▓ Armhole

Dec 2 sts at beg and end of next 3 RS rows by replacing the inc with k2tog—67 (73, 79) sts. Thereafter dec 2 sts every 4 rows 3 times by omitting the inc at beg and end of these rows—55 (61, 67) sts. Work evenly until armhole measures approx 8 (8, 8½)"/20 (20, 21)cm, binding off after nearest Row 4 of pattern.

FRONT

Work as for Back.

FINISHING

Join at point of shoulder. Join side seams. ▓

Stitch patterns can sometimes be used in shaping a garment.

The diagonal striping in this vest gently enhances the feminine shape.

野呂 85

Zamora Bolero

This little cardigan has a raglan construction but is worked back and forth on straight needles. The expanding ribbing at the bottom and sleeve edges lends a feminine touch. For a longer body or sleeves, simply keep knitting until your desired length.

Sizes
S (M, M2, L)

Finished Measurements
▧ Bust 35 (36¾, 38½, 40¼)"/90 (93.5, 98, 102)cm

▧ Length 15½ (16, 17, 18)"/39.5 (40.5, 43, 46)cm

Yarn
300 (300, 400, 400)g *Kochoran* #12

Needles
One pair size 9 (6mm) straight needles *or size to obtain gauge*

Gauge
14 sts/20 rows = 4"/10cm in St st
Take time to check gauge.

BODY
Cast on 125 (131, 137, 143) sts and work in St st for 5½"/14cm (all sizes), ending with a WS row.

Next row (RS) K27 (29, 30, 31) sts, bind off 8 (8, 9, 10) sts, k55 (57, 59, 61) sts, bind off 8 (8, 9, 10)sts, k27 (29, 30, 31) sts.

Next row (WS) P27 (29, 30, 31) sts, cast on 36 (38, 40, 42)sts, p55 (57, 59, 61), cast on 36 (38, 40, 42) sts, p27 (29, 30, 31) sts— 181 (191, 199, 207) sts.

Work 4 (6, 8, 10) rows.

▧ Raglan shaping
K24 (26, 27, 28) sts, k2tog tbl, sl 1 p-wise, k2tog, k32 (34, 36, 38)sts, k2tog tbl, sl 1 p-wise, k2tog, 49 (51, 53, 55) sts, k2tog tbl, sl 1 p-wise, k2tog, k32 (34, 36, 38)sts, k2tog tbl, sl 1 p-wise, k2tog, k24 (26, 27, 28) sts— 173 (183, 191, 199) sts.

Work 3 rows evenly, purling the sl st on WS rows and slipping on RS rows.

Zamora Bolero continued

Dec 1 st at either side of each sl st every 4 rows 0 (0, 1, 1) time, then every 2 rows 12 times (all sizes)—77 (87, 87, 95).

Work 2 rows evenly. Bind off all sts over next row.

EDGING
▥ Sleeves

With RS facing, pick up 43 (43, 48, 48) sts evenly spaced along cast-on edge of sleeve. Work Rib pattern as follows:

Row 1 (WS) K2, * p4, k1*, rep between * * across row, ending with k1.

Row 2 (RS) P2, *k4, p1*, rep between * * across row, ending with p1.

Repeat these 2 rows once.

Inc row (WS) K2, *p4, m1, k1, m1*, rep between * * across row, ending with p4, k2.

Next row (RS) P2, *k4, p3*, rep between * * across row, ending with k4, p2.

Work in Rib pattern until edging measures 3½"/9cm or desired length. Bind off all sts over next row.

▥ Body

With RS facing and starting at Left Front cast-on edge, pick up 131 (131, 136, 143) sts evenly spaced along bottom edge.

Row 1 (WS) P5, * k1 p4*, rep between * * across row, ending with k1, p5.

Row 2 (RS) P5, * p1, k4*, rep between * *

across row, ending with k1, p5.

Repeat these 2 rows once.

Inc row (WS) P5, * m1, k1, m1, p4*, rep between * * across row, ending with m1, k1, m1, p5.

Next row (RS) K5, *p3, k4*, rep between * * across row, ending with p3, k5.

Work in Rib pattern until edging measures 3"/8 cm or desired length. Bind off all sts over next row.

FINISHING

Join side of rib edging to armhole. Join sleeve edging, fitting into armhole. ◼

Jiutepec Cardigan

Once again, long buttonholes create texture and visual interest (see Ekeby Vest on page 34 and Dorotea Pullover on page 54). This time the buttonhole rows are worked in *Iro* with rows of contrasting *Silk Garden* worked loosely in between.

Sizes
S (M, L)

Finished Measurements
▦ Bust 34 (40, 46)"/86 (101.5, 117)cm
▦ Length 25 (27½, 30)"/63.5 (70, 76)cm

Yarn
300 (400, 400)g *Iro* #9 (MC)
200 (200, 200)g *Iro* #47 (CC)
150 (200, 250)g *Silk Garden* #47

Needles
One pair size 11 (7 mm) straight needles
or size to obtain gauge

Gauge
12 sts/18 rows = 4"/10cm with *Silk Garden* in St st
Take time to check gauge.

NOTES
▦ Instead of *Iro*, this pattern can be knit in *Silk Garden Chunky* using the same amount of yarn and needle size.

▦ If you wish to add buttons to this cardigan, work the last 4 rows of the Left Front in Gst with *Iro* (MC). This makes a more stable edge for placing buttons. Use the holes on the Right Front edge as buttonholes.

HOLE STRIPE PATTERN
▦ Hole Stripe A
Row 1 (RS) With *Silk Garden*, knit.
Row 2 (WS) Purl.
Row 3 (RS) With *Iro* (MC), knit.
Row 4 (WS) K2, *bind off 4 sts, k4, rep from *, end with k2.
Row 5 (RS) K2, *cast on 4 sts, k4, rep from *, end with k2.
Row 6 (WS) Knit.
Row 7 (RS) With *Silk Garden*, knit.
Row 8 (WS) Purl.

Jiutepec Cardigan continued

Hole Stripe B
Row 1 (RS) With *Silk Garden*, knit.
Row 2 (WS) Purl.
Row 3 (RS) With *Iro* (MC), knit.
Row 4 (WS) K6, *bind off 4 sts, k4, rep from *, end with k6.
Row 5 (RS) K6, *cast on 4 sts, k4, rep from *, end with k6.
Row 6 (WS) Knit.
Row 7 (RS) With *Silk Garden*, knit.
Row 8 (WS) Purl.

RIGHT FRONT
With *Iro* (MC), cast on 56 (64, 72) sts and work Stripe A starting with Row 3. Continue in Stripe B. Cast on 1 sts at end of Row 4 and every other row at neck edge, 2 times; 3 sts once and 6 sts once (all sizes). Incorporate the new sts into the existing Stripe pattern.
Size small Work Stripe A and Stripe B a total of 2 times, then Stripe A once more.
Size medium Work Stripe A and Stripe B a total of 3 times.
Size large Work Stripe A and Stripe B a total of 3 times, then Stripe A once more.
All sizes Piece measures approx 7½ [9, 10½]"/19 [23, 26.5]cm from cast-on edge.

Armhole (all sizes)
Next row (RS) Bind off 23 (25, 27) sts. Work on rem sts, alternating the Stripe patterns as above for approx 3"/8cm (or 2 *Iro* Stripes). Cast on 23 (25, 27) sts.

BACK
Continue working in Stripes beg with Stripe B (Stripe A, Stripe B).
Size small Thereafter rep Stripes A and B, 4 times.
Size medium Thereafter Stripes B and A, 4 times, then Stripe B once more.
Size large Thereafter Stripes A and B, 5 times.

Armhole
Next row (RS) Bind off 23 (25, 27) sts. Work on rem sts, alternating the Stripe patterns as above for approx 3"/8 cm (or 2 *Iro* Stripes). Cast on 23 (25, 27) sts.

LEFT FRONT
Size small Work Stripes A and B once.
Size medium Work Stripe B, then Stripes A and B once.
Size large Work Stripes A and B twice.
All sizes Work rows 1–6 of Stripe A.
Next row (RS) Bind off at neck edge every other row, 6 sts once, 3 sts once and 1 st 3 times. Continue to work evenly rest of Stripe B and then Stripe A through Row 5. Bind off all sts in knit over next row.

Jiutepec Cardigan

SLEEVES

(All sizes) Cast on 12 sts with *Silk Garden* and knit 1 row.

Next row Purl, cast on 11 sts at end of row.

Next row Knit.

Repeat these 2 rows 3 more times.

Change to *Iro* (MC) and Hole Stripe patterns.

Size small Repeat Pattern A and Pattern B 3 times.

Size medium Repeat Pattern A and Pattern B 3 times, then Pattern A once more.

Size large Rep Pattern A and Pattern B 4 times.

All sizes

Next row (RS) Bind off 11 sts, work to end.

Next row (WS) Purl.

Rep these 2 rows 3 more times or to desired length.

Bind off all sts over next row.

SLEEVE EDGING

With *Iro* (MC), pick up 31 (36, 41) sts at bottom of Sleeve and work Gst for 4 rows.

Change to *Iro* (CC) and work as follows:

▥ Rib St Pattern

Row 1 (RS) With *Iro* (CC), p1, k4 across row, ending with p1.

Row 2 (WS) K1, p4 across row, ending with k1.

Row 3 (RS) P1, k4 across row, ending with p1.

Row 4 (WS) K1, * m1, p4, m1, k1, rep from * across row.

Row 5 (RS) P2, k4, * p3, k4, rep from *, ending with p2.

Repeat Rows 4 and 5 3 more times or to desired length. Bind off all sts over next row.

BODY EDGING

With *Iro* (MC), pick up 96 (116, 136) sts at bottom of Body and work Gst for 4 rows.

Change to *Iro* (CC) and work as follows:

▥ Rib St Pattern

Row 1 (RS) With *Iro* (CC), p1, k4 across row, ending with p1.

Row 2 (WS) K1, p4 across row, ending with k1.

Row 3 (RS) P1, k4 across row, ending with p1.

Row 4 (WS) K1, * m1, p4, m1, k1, rep from * across row.

Row 5 (RS) P2, k4, * p3, k4, rep from *, ending with p2.

Repeat Rows 4 and 5 6 more times. Bind off all sts over next row.

COLLAR EDGING

With *Iro* (MC), pick up 46 (46, 46) sts around Collar and work Gst for 4 rows.

Change to *Iro* (CC) and work in Rib St pattern as for Sleeve edging.

▒ Rib St Pattern

Row 1 (RS) With *Iro* (CC), p1, k4 across row, ending with p1.

Row 2 (WS) K1, p4 across row, ending with k1.

Row 3 (RS) P1, k4 across row, ending with p1.

Row 4 (WS) K1, p4 across row, ending with k1.

Row 5 (RS) P1, k4 across row, ending with p1.

Row 6 (WS) K1, * m1, p4, m1, k1, rep from * across row.

Row 7 (RS) P2, k4, * p3, k4, rep from *, ending with p2.

Repeat Rows 4 and 5 6 more times or to desired length. Bind off all sts over next row. ▪

Rikardis Tunic

The pattern of solid-colored squares that frames the pieces in this tunic is inspired by details on suits of armor from times gone by. The slightly thicker *Cash Iroha* is worked at the same gauge as *Silk Garden Lite,* lending stability to the edgings.

▬▬▬▬▬

Sizes
S (M, M2, L)

Finished Measurements
▪ Bust 34 (38, 42, 46)"/86.5 (96.5, 107, 117)cm
▪ Length 27½ (28, 28½, 29)"/70 (71, 72.5, 73.5)cm

Yarn
400 (450, 500, 550)g *Silk Garden Lite* (SGL) #2013
100 (100, 150, 150)g *Cash Iroha* (CI) #112

Needles
One pair size 6 (4mm) straight needles
or size to obtain gauge

Gauges
20 sts/30 rows = 4"/10cm with SGL in St st
20 sts/40 rows = 4"/10cm with CI in St st
Take time to check gauge.

NOTE
Yarns are carried along at back of work.

BOTTOM PIECES (make two)
With CI, cast on 122 (130, 138, 146) sts and work 6 rows of Garter st.

Row 1 (RS) K3 sts with SGL, *k4 with CI, k4 with SGL*, rep between * *, k4 with CI, k3 with SGL.

Row 2 (WS) P3 sts with SGL, *k4 with CI, p4 with SGL*, rep between * *, end with k4 with CI, p3 with SGL.

Repeat these 2 rows 2 more times.

Continue now in St st with SGL until piece measures 15"/38cm (all sizes). Bind off all sts.

BODICE FRONT
With CI, cast on 90 (98, 106, 114) sts and work 6 rows in Gst.

Row 1 (RS) K3 sts wth SGL, *k4 with CI, k4 with SGL*, rep between * *, k4 with CI, k3 with SGL.

野呂

Row 2 (WS) P 3 sts with SGL, *k4 with CI, p4 with SGL*, rep between * *, k4 with CI, p3 with SGL.

Repeat these 2 rows 2 more times.

Continue now in St st with SGL until piece measures 6½ (7, 7½, 8)"/16.5 (18, 19, 20)cm. Inc 1 st at each side every 4 rows 14 times (incs are worked inside the 2 outermost sts). After first side inc and on next WS row, place Marker B 28 (32, 36, 40) sts in from right edge, and Marker A 28 (32, 36, 40) sts in from left edge (there are 36 sts between markers for neck opening—all sizes).

BOTTOM OF NECK OPENING
(Front and Back)

Rows 1, 3 and 5 (RS) Work in SGL to Marker A, *k4 with CI, k4 with SGL*, rep between * * 3 more times (Back: 5 more times), k4 with CI , finish row with SGL.

Rows 2, 4 and 6 (WS) Work in SGL to Marker B, *k4 with CI, p4 with SGL*, rep between * * 3 more times (Back: 5 more times), k4 with CI, finish row with SGL.

Row 7 (RS) Knit in SGL until 6 sts remain before Marker A, k2tog tbl, place Marker C, change to CI and knit between Markers C and B, knit 4 more sts with CI, place Marker D, with SGL k2tog, knit to end of row.

Rows 8 and 10 (WS) Purl in SGL to Marker D, change to CI and knit to Marker C, change to SGL and purl to end of row.

Rows 9 and 11 (RS) Knit in SGL to Marker C, change to CI and knit to Marker D, change to SGL and knit to end of row.

Row 12 (WS) Purl in SGL until 2 sts left before Marker D, p2tog, change to CI and k8, bind off 28 sts (Back: 44 sts), k8, change to SGL and P2tog, purl to end of row.

Work each side of neck separately. Continue with incs at sides as described above.

LEFT SIDE OF NECK OPENING

Rows 1, 3 and 5 (RS) Knit in SGL to 4 sts past Marker C, change to CI and k4 sts.

Rows 2, 4 and 6 (WS) K4 sts in CI, change to SGL and purl to end.

Row 7 (RS) Knit in SGL until 2 sts before Marker C, k2tog tbl, change to CI and k8 sts.

Rows 8 and 10 (WS) K8 sts in CI, change to SGL and purl to end of row.

Row 9 and 11 (RS) Knit in SGL to Marker C, change to CI and k8 sts.

Row 12 (WS) K8 sts in CI, change to SGL and p2tog, purl to end of row.

Repeat these 12 rows 2 more times. Then rep Rows 1–4. Bind off all sts over next row.

RIGHT SIDE OF NECK OPENING

With new yarn and starting at neck edge, work as follows:

Rows 1, 3 and 5 (RS) K4 sts in CI, change to SGL and knit to end.

Rows 2, 4 and 6 (WS) Purl in SGL to 4 sts past Marker D, change to CI and k4 sts.

Row 7 (RS) K8 sts in CI, change to SGL and k2tog, knit to end of row.

Row 8 and 10 (WS) Purl in SGL to Marker D, change to CI and k8 sts.

Row 9 and 11 (RS) K8 sts in CI, change to SGL and purl to end of row.

Row 12 (WS) Purl in SGL until 2 sts before Marker D, p2tog, change to CI and k8 sts.

Repeat these 12 rows 2 more times. Then rep Rows 1–4.

Bind off all sts over next row.

BODICE BACK

Cast on and work as for Bodice Front for 6½ (7, 7½, 8)"/16.5 (18, 19, 20)cm. Inc 1 st at each side every 4 rows, 14 times. Work until piece measures 12"/30cm, ending with a WS row. Place Markers A and B at each side of the middle 52 sts (all sizes). Work each side of neck separately.

Work Bottom of Neck Opening. Work Rows 1–4 of Left Side of Neck Opening. Bind off all sts.

With new yarn and starting at neck edge, work Rows 1–4 of Right Side of Neck Opening. Bind off all sts.

SLEEVES (make 2)

With Cash Iroha, cast on 74 (82, 90, 98) sts and work 6 rows in Gst.

Row 1 (RS) K3 sts wth SGL, *k4 with CI, k4 with SGL*, rep between * *, end k4 with CI, k3 with SGL.

Row 2 (WS) P3 sts with SGL, *k4 with CI, p4 with SGL*, rep between * *, end k4 with CI, p3 with SGL.

Repeat these 2 rows 2 more times.

Continue now in St st with SGL until piece measures 7"/18cm (all sizes). Bind off all sts.

FINISHING

Join shoulder seams. Fit sleeve along side edge and join. Join sleeve and side seams. Join side seams of bottom pieces. Run a thread along the cast-off edge of Bottom pieces and gather slightly to fit along bottom edge of Bodice. Place the cast-off edge of the Bottom pieces under the cast-on edge of the Bodice. Join the Bottom to the Bodice along Row 6 of the *Cash Iroha* Gst edging. ■

Adhara Brimmed Cap

The triangular color sections in the crown of this fun newsboy cap make good use of Kureyon's natural striping. The crown is worked using short rows to form a circle. Notice how the colors flow nicely from wedge to wedge around the crown.

Size
Adult

Finished Measurements
Circumference 22"/56cm

Yarn
100g *Kureyon* #180

Needles
One pair size 6 (5.5 mm) straight needles *or size to obtain gauge*

Gauge
16 sts/22 rows = 4"/10cm in St st
Take time to check gauge.

STRIPED WEDGE PATTERN
Row 1 (RS) Purl.
Row 2 (WS) Knit.
Row 3 Knit.
Row 4 P1, *k2tog, yo, rep from *, end with p1.
Row 5 Knit.
Row 6 Knit.
Row 7 Purl.
Row 8 Purl.
Row 9 K7, turn work, sl 1 p-wise with yarn in front, p6.
Row 10 K15, turn work, sl 1 p-wise wyf, p14.
Row 11 K23, turn work, sl 1 p-wise wyf, p22.
Row 12 K31, turn work, sl 1 p-wise wyf, p30.
Row 13 K23, turn work, sl 1 p-wise wyf, p22.
Row 14 K15, turn work, sl 1 p-wise wyf, p14.
Row 15 K7, turn work, sl 1 p-wise wyf, p6.
Row 16 Knit—34 sts.
Row 17 Purl.
Repeat Rows 1–17.

CROWN

Cast on 34 sts and work according to Striped Wedge patt above for 8 repeats. Bind off.

EDGING

Along right-hand edge, pick up 104 sts (13 sts for every repeat of Striped Wedge patt).

Next row Knit, dec 32 sts (k2tog) evenly spaced across row (4 decs in each repeat of Striped Wedge patt)—72 sts.

Work 7 rows in Gst. Bind off.

BRIM

Cast on 30 sts and work 8 rows in Gst. Dec 1 st at each side every 2 rows 4 times. Thereafter bind off 2 sts at beg of every row, 4 times. K 2 rows. Cast on 2 sts at beg of every row 4 times. Thereafter inc 1 st at each side every 2 rows 4 times. K 8 rows. Bind off all sts.

FINISHING

Join seam at back. Weave a piece of yarn through holes at top edge of cap and pull tight. Fasten off. To form knob at top, wrap a piece of yarn several times around the hat 2½"/6cm from top, pulling tightly. Fasten off. Fold brim in half, RS to RS, and join at edges. Turn brim inside out and pin to center front of cap. Join at bind-off row of edging. ■

Alegria
Sleeveless Sweater

The curved edging knit in *Cash Iroha* dresses up this feminine top and complements the shaped waist. *Silver Thaw* is so soft you can wear it directly against your skin.

Sizes
S (M, L)

Finished Measurements
■ Bust 32¼ (35, 36½)/82 (88, 93)cm
■ Length 19¾ (21, 21¾)"/50 (53, 55)cm

Yarn
Approx 100 (100, 100)g *Cash Iroha* #2
Approx 150 (200, 200)g *Silver Thaw* #02

Needles
One pair size 8 (5mm) straight needles
or size to obtain gauge
One 30"/80cm size 7 (4.5mm) circular needle
Size 7 (4.5mm) double-pointed needles

Gauge
16 sts/22 rows = 4"/10cm with *Silver Thaw* and size 8 (5mm) needles in reverse St st
Take time to check gauge.

NOTE
■ Work all incs and decs inside the 2 outermost sts.

■ If you have trouble locating *Silver Thaw*, this pattern can be knit in *Kureyon* using the same amount of yarn and size needles.

I-CORD
All rows Knit 3 sts, slip sts back to left-hand needle.

BACK
With size 8 (5mm) straight needles and *Silver Thaw*, cast on 66 (70, 74) sts and work in Reverse St st. Dec 1 st at each side every 4 rows 4 times. When piece measures 5½ (6, 6¼)"/14 (15, 16)cm, inc 1 st at each side every 6 rows, 4 times.

■ Armhole
When piece measures 12½ (13, 13½)"/32 (33, 34)cm, bind off 4 (4, 4) sts at beg of next 2 rows. Thereafter bind off 1 st every 4 rows 12

(14, 16) times. *At same time*: When armhole measures 3¼ (3½, 4)"/ 8 (9, 10)cm, work back neck shaping as follows: Divide work. Bind off 1 st from neck edge every other row 13 (13, 13) times. Bind off all sts when piece measures 20 (21, 21¾)"/(51 (53, 55)cm. Work other side of neck opening in the same way, reversing the shaping.

FRONT
Cast on and work as for Back until Armhole.

▥ Armhole
Divide work. Working each side separately, bind off at armhole edge as for Back. *At same time*: Bind off 1 st at neck edge every other row 7 times and then every 4 rows 6 times. When piece measures 20 (21, 21½)"/51 (53) 55cm, bind off all sts. Work other side of neck opening in the same way, reversing the shaping.

NECK EDGING
Join left shoulder seam. With RS facing and with size 7 (4.5 mm) circular needle and *Cash Iroha*, pick up 87 (90, 93) sts evenly spaced around neck opening, starting at right side of back neck. Knit 3 rows.

▥ Loops
With double-pointed needles, work an I-cord of first 3 sts for 11 rows. *Bend the I-cord over to the left without twisting and k tog the first st from the double-pointed needle with the first st on the circular needle. K tog the 2nd sts and the 3rd sts the same way. Continue now on these 3 sts with the double-pointed needles in I-cord for 11 rows. Repeat from * until all sts are worked. Fasten off. Join right shoulder seam.

ARMHOLE EDGING
Starting at bottom with RS facing, size 7 (4.5 mm) circular needle and *Cash Iroha*, pick up 57 (60, 63) sts evenly spaced around armhole opening and knit 3 rows. Work Loops as described for Neck Edging.

Join side seams.

With RS facing, size 7 (4.5 mm) circular needle and *Cash Iroha*, pick up 126 (138, 150) sts evenly spaced along bottom of Front and Back. Work 3 rows in Gst. Work Loops as described for Neck Edging.

Join edges of the loops. ■

Kolsva Scoopneck Pullover

The plunging neckline of this sweater highlights the soft, feminine characteristics of *Kochoran*. The garment is fitted and lightly shaped to further enhance the effect of the yarn. It is casual enough to wear with jeans or elegant enough for evening.

Sizes
S (M, L, XL)

Finished Measurements
▓ Bust Approx 36 (38, 40, 42)"/91.5 (96.5, 101.5, 106.5)cm
▓ Length Approx 20½ (21, 21½, 22)"/52 (53, 54.5, 56)cm

Yarn
Approx 400 (500, 500, 600)g *Kochoran* #14

Needles
One pair size 9 (6mm) straight needles
or size to obtain gauge
One 30"/80cm size 9 (6mm) circular needle
or size to obtain gauge

Gauge
14 sts/20 rows = 4"/10cm
square in St st
Take time to check gauge.

NOTES
▓ When only one number is indicated in pattern, it is for all sizes.
▓ Incs and decs should be worked inside the selvage st at each edge.

RIB STITCH
Row 1 *K2, p2, repeat from * across row, ending with k2.
Row 2 *P2, k2, repeat from *, ending with p2.

BACK
Cast on 64 (68, 72, 76) sts. Work in Rib st rib for 6 rows. Knit 1 row.

Next row (RS) Change to St st beg with a purl row. Work 4 rows. Dec 1 st at each end of next row. Work decs again every 6 rows twice. Work evenly until piece measures 5¾ (6, 6¼, 6½)"/14.5 (15, 16, 16.5)cm. Inc 1 st at each end of next row. Work incs again every 8 rows twice. Work evenly until piece measures 14"/35.5cm (all sizes).

▨ Armhole
Bind off at each armhole edge every other row 3 sts once, 2 sts once and 1 st once (once, once, twice). Work evenly until piece measures 20 (20½, 21, 21½)"/51 (52, 53, 54.5)cm.

▨ Shoulder Shaping
Bind off 7 (8, 8, 9) sts at beg of next 2 rows, then 6 (7, 8, 8) sts at beg of next 2 rows. Bind off rem 26 (26, 28, 28) sts.

FRONT
Cast on and work as for Back until piece measures 12"/30.5 cm (all sizes).

▨ Front Neck
Next row (RS) Work 28 (30, 31, 33) sts, bind off middle 8 (8, 10, 10) sts, finish row. Work each side of neck opening separately. At neck edge bind off 4 (4, 4, 4) sts once, 2 (2, 2, 2) sts once, 1 st 2 (2, 3, 3) times. Work evenly for 4 rows. Bind off 1 (1, 1, 1) st at neck edge.
At same time: When piece measures 14"/35.5cm, work armhole shaping.

▨ Armhole
At beg of next WS row, bind off 3 sts once, 2 sts once and 1 st once (once, once, twice). Work evenly until piece measures 20 (20½, 21, 21½)"/51 (52, 53, 54.5)cm.

▨ Shoulder Shaping
From shoulder edge and every other row, bind off 7 (8, 8, 9) sts once, then 6 (7, 8, 8) sts once. Work other side of neck opening in the same way, reversing the shaping.

SLEEVES
Cast on 38 (38, 42, 42) sts and work in Rib st for 6 rows. Knit 1 row.

Next row (RS) Change to St st beg with a purl row. Inc 1 st at each edge every 8 rows, 4 (5, 4, 5) times. Work evenly until piece measures 12½ (13, 13½ 14)"/32 (33, 34, 35)cm.

▨ Sleeve Cap
Bind off at each side 3 (3, 3, 3) sts once and 2 (2, 2, 2) sts once. Thereafter bind off 1 st every 4 rows 3 (3, 3, 3) times, then every 2 rows 6 (6, 6, 6) times. Bind off 2 sts at beg of next 4 (4, 6, 6) rows. Bind off rem sts.

FINISHING
Join shoulder and side seams. Starting at the right side of back neck, pick up 24 sts across back neck, pick up 110 sts evenly spaced around front neck opening. Work in Rib st for approx 6"/15cm. Bind off all sts. Fold ribbing to inside and join. Join sleeve seams. Fit sleeves into armholes and join. ▪

Margareta
Shoulder Bag

This is the second bag I designed using what I call the "origami" approach (see Lotorp Origami Bag on page 38). It is worked in *Silk Garden Chunky* in one piece and folded, and then the contrasting *Silk Mountain* rectangle is sewn in place.

Finished Measurements
- Width 12"/30cm
- Length (not including strap) 15¾"/40cm

Yarn
300g *Silk Garden Chunky* #5
50g *Silk Mountain* #14

Needles
One pair size 10 (6mm) straight needles
or size to obtain gauge

Gauges
14 sts= 4"/10cm with *Silk Mountain*
16 sts= 4"/10cm with *Silk Garden Chunky*
Take time to check gauge.

NOTES
- Bag is worked in one piece with *Silk Garden Chunky*. *Silk Mountain* rectangle is worked separately.
- Bag can also be worked with *Iro* using the same amount of yarn and needle size.

BAG
With *Silk Garden Chunky*, cast on 60 sts and work Seed st for 4"/10cm.
Bind off 16 sts at beg of next 2 rows—28 sts.
Work evenly for 4"/10cm.
Cast on 16 sts at end of next 2 rows—60 sts.
Work evenly for 4"/10cm.
Bind off 22 sts at beg of next 2 rows—16 sts.
Work evenly for 11½"/29cm.
Cast on 22 sts at end of next 2 rows—60 sts.
Work evenly for 4"/10cm.
Bind off 16 sts at beg of next 2 rows—28 sts.
Work evenly for 4"/10cm.
Cast on 16 sts at end of next 2 rows—60 sts.
Work evenly for 4"/10cm.
Bind off 22 sts at beg of next 2 rows—16 sts.

SHOULDER STRAP
Continue working over rem 16 sts for approx 34"/86cm or desired to length.
Bind off all sts.

Margareta Shoulder Bag continued

RECTANGLE (make 2)
With *Silk Mountain*, cast on 28 sts. Work in garter st until piece measures 4¼"/11cm. Bind off.

FINISHING
Line up edges with same letter with each other according to diagram and seam. Place the *Silk Mountain* rectangles in the respective empty rectangles of the bag on each side and seam into place. Try on bag and adjust strap length as desired. Join to center of cast-on edge of bag. ■

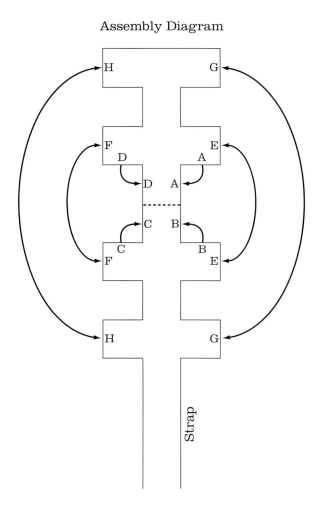

Assembly Diagram

Origami shaping is a really fun way to make the most of colorful striping and distinctive textures when knitting bags.

Josefina Scalloped Sweater

Like the Rikardis short-sleeved tunic (see page 94), this pullover was inspired by medieval armor, but with a very different result. Knit side to side, the contrasting *Cash Iroha* stripes are striking against the multicolored *Niji*. Feminine and soft, it is a pleasure to knit and to wear.

Sizes
S (M, L)

Finished Measurements
▦ Bust 34 (38, 42)"/86 (96.5, 107)cm
▦ Length 20 (21, 22)"/51 (53.5, 56)cm

Yarn
200 (200, 200)g *Cash Iroha* #2
200 (250, 300)g *Niji* #261

Needles
One pair size 10 (6mm) straight needles
or size to obtain gauge

Gauge
14 sts/20 rows = 4"/10cm in St st in *Cash Iroha* held double or *Niji* worked single
Take time to check gauge.

NOTES
▦ This pullover is knit from side to side.
▦ If you have trouble locating *Niji*, this pattern can be knit in *Kochoran* using the same amount of yarn and size needles.

FRONT
▦ **Left Shoulder**

With *Cash Iroha* held double, cast on 68 (71, 74) sts. Knit 1 row. Purl 1 row. Knit 1 row.

Row 1 (RS) With *Niji*, knit 68 (71, 74) sts, cast on 4 new sts at end of row—72 (75, 78) sts.

Rows 2–11 Work in St st, starting with a purl row.

Row 12 (WS) Bind off 4 sts, work to end.

Rows 13 and 15 With *Cash Iroha*, knit.

Rows 14 and 16 With *Cash Iroha*, purl.

Repeat rows 1–12, once more.

Josefina Scalloped Sweater continued

Left Side of Neck Opening

Next row (RS) With *Niji*, bind off 14 sts. Change to *Cash Iroha* and knit to end of row. Work 3 more rows in St st, starting with a purl row.

Row 1 (RS) With *Niji*, knit 54 (57, 60) sts. Cast on 4 sts at end of row.

Row 2 Knit. Cast on 2 sts at end of row.

Rows 3–11 Work in St st, starting with a purl row.

Row 12 Bind off 4 sts, finish row.

Row 13 Bind off 2 sts. Change to *Cash Iroha* and knit to end of row.

Rows 14 and 16 With *Cash Iroha*, purl.

Row 15 With *Cash Iroha*, knit.

Repeat Rows 1–16 2 more times.

Right Side of Neck Opening

Row 1 With *Niji*, knit 54 (57, 60) sts. Cast on 4 sts at end of row.

Row 2 Knit. Cast on 14 sts at end of row— 72 (75, 78) sts.

Rows 3–11 Work in St st, starting with a purl row.

Row 12 Bind off 4 sts, finish row.

Rows 13 and 15 With *Cash Iroha*, knit.

Rows 14 and 16 With *Cash Iroha*, purl.

Right Shoulder

Row 1 (RS) With *Niji*, knit 68 (71, 74) sts. Cast on 4 sts at end of row.

Rows 2–11 Work in St st, starting with a knit row.

Row 12 Bind off 4 sts, finish row.

Row 13 Change to *Cash Iroha*, knit.

Row 14 Purl.

Row 15 Knit.

Row 16 Purl.

Bind off all sts over next row.

BACK

Left Shoulder

With *Cash Iroha* held double, cast on 66 (69, 72) sts. Knit 1 row. Purl 1 row. Knit 1 row.

Row 1 (RS) With *Niji*, knit 66 (69, 72) sts, cast on 4 new sts at end of row—72 (75, 78) sts.

Rows 2–11 Work in St st, starting with a knit row.

Row 12 (WS) Bind off 4 sts, work to end.

Row 13 and 15 With *Cash Iroha*, knit.

Row 14 and 16 With *Cash Iroha*, purl.

Size small Rep Rows 1–12 once more. Bind off all sts.

Sizes medium and large Rep Rows 1–16 once, then Rows 1–12 once. Bind off all sts.

Left Shoulder

With *Niji*, bind off 2 sts at beg of row. Change to *Cash Iroha* and knit 66 (69, 72) sts. Purl 1 row. Knit 1 row. Purl 1 row.

Row 1 (RS) With *Niji*, knit 66 (69, 72) sts, cast

on 4 new sts at end of row—70 (73, 76) sts.

Row 2 Knit. Cast on 2 sts at end of row.

Rows 3–11 Work in St st, starting with a purl row.

Row 12 (WS) Bind off 4 sts, work to end.

Row 13 Bind off 2 sts. Change to *Cash Iroha*, knit to end of row.

Row 14 and 16 Purl.

Row 15 Knit.

(All sizes) Rep Rows 1–16 twice.

■ **Right Side of Neck Opening and Shoulder**

Row 1 (RS) With *Niji*, knit. Cast on 4 sts at end of row—70 (73, 76) sts.

Row 2 Knit. Cast on 2 sts at end of row.

Rows 3–11 Work in St st, starting with a purl row.

Row 12 (WS) Bind off 4 sts, work to end.

Row 13 and 15 With *Cash Iroha*, knit.

Rows 14 and 16 With *Cash Iroha*, purl.

Size small Rep Rows 1–16 once more. Bind off all sts.

Sizes medium and large Rep Rows 1–16 twice. Bind off all sts.

SLEEVES

With *Cash Iroha*, cast on 50 (53, 56) sts. Knit 1 row. Purl 1 row. Knit 1 row.

Row 1 (RS) With *Niji*, knit. Cast on 4 sts at end of row—54 (57, 60) sts.

Rows 2–11 Work in St st, starting with a knit row.

Row 12 Bind off 4 sts, finish row.

Row 13 Change to *Cash Iroha*, knit.

Rows 14 and 16 Purl.

Row 15 Knit.

All sizes Repeat Rows 1–16, 4 (5, 6) more times. Repeat Rows 1–14 one more time. Bind off all sts over next row.

FINISHING

Join shoulder seams. Fit sleeves to armholes and join. Join sleeve and side seams. ■

Eleonore Scarf and Hat

The same ruffle I used on the Sursa Shawl (see page 72) runs the length of the entire scarf and along the side seam of the hat, adding a decorative touch. The cashmere in both *Cashmere Island* and *Cash Iroha* will make this set a favorite.

Size
Adult

Finished Measurements
▥ Scarf length 98"/248cm
▥ Hat circumference 21½"/54.5cm

Yarn
▥ Hat
50g *Cashmere Island* #5
50g *Cash Iroha* #112
▥ Scarf
100g *Cashmere Island* #5
100g *Cash Iroha* #112

Needles
One pair each size 6 and 8 (4 and 5mm) straight needles *or size to obtain gauge*
Two 30"/80cm size 8 (5mm) circular needles for scarf *or size to obtain gauge*

Gauges
18 sts = 4"/10cm in Gst with *Cashmere Island* and size 6 (4mm) needles
16 sts = 4"/10cm in St st with *Cash Iroha* and size 6 (5mm) needles
Take time to check gauge.

NOTE
If you have trouble locating *Cashmere Island*, this pattern can be knit in *Silk Garden Lite* or *Chirimen* using the same amount of yarn and size needles.

HAT
With *Cashmere Island* and size 6 (4mm) needles, cast on 98 sts. Work in Gst for 4⅓"/11cm.
Dec row (RS) K1, knit tog every 11th and 12th st across row, end with k1—8 decs.
Knit 1 row.
Rep these 2 rows, with 1 fewer st between each dec on each dec row.
When 10 sts rem, break yarn and pull through the open sts. Tie off.

Ruffle

With RS facing, size 8 (5mm) needles and *Cash Iroha*, pick up 1 st every 4 rows along seam edge.

Row 1 (WS) *P1, yo, rep from * to end.

Row 2 (RS) Knit.

Row 3 Purl.

Row 4 *K2, make 1, rep from * to end.

Cont in St st for 5 more rows. Bind of all sts over next row.

Join seam.

SCARF

With *Cashmere Island* and size 6 (4mm) needles, cast on 24 sts and work in Gst until there is no more yarn. Bind off over next row.

Ruffle

With *Cash Iroha* and size 8 (5mm) circular needle, pick up 1 st every 4 rows along one side edge. When you have picked up along half the length of the scarf, cont with second circular needle.

Row 1 (WS) *P1, yo, rep from * to end.

Row 2 (RS) Knit.

Row 3 Purl.

Row 4 *K2, make 1, rep from * to end.

Cont in St st for 10 more rows. Bind off all sts over next row. ∎

Ulfhild Dog Sweater

A colorful sleeveless sweater with a foldover collar and button front would get any little dog's tail wagging. But worked in lace, it becomes something for the pooch that has everything!

Size
Small dog (e.g., Jack Russell, miniature poodle)

Finished Measurements
▓ Length (with collar turned down) 10½"/26.5cm
▓ Body circumference (without edgings) 17"/43cm
▓ Collar circumference (without edgings) 12"/30.5cm

Yarn
100g *Cashmere Island* #11

Needles
One pair each size 6 and 7 (4 and 4.5mm) straight needles *or size to obtain gauge*

Gauge
18 sts= 4"/10cm with size 7 (4.5mm) needles in St st
Take time to check gauge.

NOTE
▓ This dog sweater is worked in one piece starting at the back end.

▓ If you have trouble locating *Cashmere Island*, this pattern can be knit in *Silk Garden Lite* or *Chirimen* using the same amount of yarn and size needles.

TRELLIS LACE PATTERN
(multiple of 6 + 5)
Row 1 (RS) K4, * yo, sl 1, k2tog, psso, yo, k3, rep from * to last st, k1.
Row 2 Purl.
Row 3 K1, *yo, sl 1, k2tog, psso, yo, k3, rep from * to last 4 sts, yo, sl 1, k2tog, psso, yo, k1.
Row 4 Purl.
Repeat these 4 rows throughout.

RIB STITCH
Row 1 *K2, p2, repeat from * across row, ending with k2.
Row 2 *P2, k2, repeat from *, ending with p2.

BODY

With size 6 (4mm) needles, cast on 78 sts and work in Rib st for 1¾"/4cm ending with a WS row. Change to Trellis Lace patt and size 7 (4.5mm) needles. Dec 1 st over next row. Work evenly until piece measures 6"/15cm.

▥ Shoulders

Bind off 27 sts at beg of next 2 rows. Work 2 rows. Cast on 17 sts at end of next 2 rows. Cont to work in Trellis Lace patt as established for 2¾"/7cm. Bind off all sts across next row.

LEGHOLE EDGINGS

With size 6 (4mm) needles and from RS, pick up 42 sts and work in Rib st for 5 rows. Bind off all sts over next row.

COLLAR

With size 6 (4mm) needles and from RS, pick up 58 sts and work in Rib st for 2¼"/5.5 cm. Bind off all sts over next row.

LEFT BODY EDGING

With size 6 (4mm) needles and from RS, pick up 28 sts and work in Rib st for 5 rows. Bind off all sts over next row.

RIGHT BODY EDGING

With size 6 (4mm) needles and from RS, pick up 28 sts and work in Rib st for 2 rows.

▥ Buttonhole Row

Next row P1, k2tog, yo, work 4 sts, k2tog, yo, work 4 sts, p2tog, yo, work 4 sts, k2tog, yo, work 4 sts, p2tog, yo, k2.
Work 2 more rows. Bind off all sts over next row.

LEFT COLLAR EDGING

With size 6 (4mm) needles and from RS, pick up 16 sts and work in Rib st for 5 rows. Bind off all sts over next row.

RIGHT COLLAR EDGING

With size 6 (4mm) needles and from RS, pick up 16 sts and work in Rib st for 2 rows.

▥ Buttonhole Row

Next row P1, k2tog, yo, work 4 sts, k2tog, yo, work 4 sts, p2tog, yo, k2.
Work 2 more rows. Bind off all sts over next row.

FINISHING

Sew on buttons. ▪

119

Erendira Lace Sweater

This close-fitting sweater is crocheted in *Silk Garden*, while the edgings are picked up and knit in *Silk Mountain*. The difference in the weight and structure of the yarns helps with the shaping and lends drama to the garment.

Sizes
S (M, L)

Finished Measurements
▥ Bust 34¾ (37, 39¼)"/88 (94, 100)cm
▥ Length 22 (22¾, 24)"/56 (58, 60)cm

Yarn
200 (250, 300)g *Silk Garden* #241
100 (150, 150)g *Silk Mountain* #10

Needles
On pair size 11 (8mm) straight needles *or size to obtain gauge*
One size 7 (4.5mm) crochet hook *or size to obtain gauge*

Gauge
11 sts/22 rows = 4"/10cm square in St st
Take time to check gauge.

NOTES
▥ Bear in mind when measuring the pieces before finishing that the garment will stretch lengthwise.
▥ If you have trouble locating *Silk Mountain*, this pattern can be knit in *Iro* or *Furisode* using the same amount of yarn and size needles.

CROCHET PATTERN
Row 1 (RS) Chain 6, *(1 sc, chain 3, 1 sc) in the 3rd st on the first arch, chain 5 * rep between * * 12 (13, 14) times. End with chain 2, 1 dc in the 5th chain st of the arch. Turn work.

Row 2 (WS) Chain 6, *(1sc, chain 3, 1 sc) in 3rd chain in the first big arch, chain 5 *, rep between * * 12 (13, 14) times.
Repeat Rows 2 and 3 throughout.

Erendira Lace Sweater continued

BACK
▓ Border
With *Silk Mountain* and size 11 (8mm) needles, cast on 54 (58, 62) sts. Work in Gst and dec 1 st every 10 rows 2 times (all sizes). Work evenly until piece measures 5¼"/1 cm (all sizes). Bind off over next row.

▓ Body
With *Silk Garden*, make a loop and attach to beg of bind-off row. *Chain 5, skip 4 sts, 1 sc along bind-off row of knitting *(approx every 1½"/3.5cm across row), rep between * * 13 (14, 15) times. Continue in Crochet pattern. When piece measures 20½ (21¼, 22)"/52 (54, 56)cm, break yarn at end of row.

FRONT
Cast on with *Silk Mountain* and work as for Back. Continue with *Silk Garden* and Crochet pattern until piece measures 18 (19, 19¼)"/46 (48, 50)cm, ending with a WS row.

▓ Neck Opening
Next row Work 6 (6, 7) loops (you are now at neck opening), end row with 1sc, 3 chains, 1sc, turn. Work 3 sl sts to 3rd chain of arch, then *chain 5, 1sc*. Work across row in established pattern. Dec 1 arch at neck edge in manner described above every other row until 3 (3, 4) arches remain for shoulder. Fasten off. Work other side of neck in the same way, reversing the shaping.

SLEEVES
▓ Border
With size 11 (8 mm) needles and *Silk Mountain,* cast on 30 (32, 34) sts. Work in Gst and dec 1 st at each side every 8 rows, 2 times (all sizes). Bind off when piece measures 4¾"/12 cm (all sizes).

▓ Body
With *Silk Garden* make a loop and attach to beg of bind-off row. *Chain 5, skip 4 sts, 1 sc along bind-off row of knitting * (approx every 1½"/3.5 cm across row), rep between * * 7 (8, 9) times. Continue in Crochet pattern. When piece measures 9"/23cm, inc 1 arch (2 chain, 1 dc in the 5th chain of the arch) at end of next 2 rows (all sizes). Work inc again when piece measures 13½"/34cm (all sizes). Work evenly until piece measures 17¾ (18, 18½)"/45 (46, 47)cm. Break yarn at end of row.

FINISHING
Join shoulder seams. Match middle of sleeve top to shoulder seam and join sleeve to body. Join sleeves and side seams. ▪

Skeppsta Diamond Pane Pullover

The back and front of this wide paneled pullover each comprise four panels. The diagonal pattern is created through the use of short rows in the stockinette stitch areas.

Sizes
S/M (L)

Finished Measurements
- Bust 50½ (57)"/128 (144)cm
- Length 20½ (20½)"/51 (51)cm

Yarn
Approx 700 (800)g *Transitions #6*

Needles
One pair size 13 (9mm) straight needles *or size to obtain gauge*
One 24"/60cm size 13 (9mm) circular needle *or size to obtain gauge*

Gauge
10 sts/14 rows = 4"/10cm square in St st

NOTES
- The Back is composed of four panels that are worked separately and seamed at middle. Each side of Front is two panels.
- This pattern can also be knit in *Iro* or using the same amount of yarn and size needles.

BACK
Panel A (make 2)
Cast on 18 (20) sts. Purl 1 row. Knit 1 row.

Row 1 (RS) K4 (4), sl 1 with yarn in front, turn, bring yarn to front, sl 1, p4 (4).

Row 2 K7 (8), sl 1 wyf, turn, bring yarn to front, sl 1, p7 (8).

Row 3 K11 (12), sl 1 wyf, turn, bring yarn to front, sl 1, p11 (12).

Row 4 K14 (16), sl 1 wyf, turn, bring yarn to front, sl 1, p14 (16).

Row 5 K17 (19), sl 1 wyf, turn, bring yarn to front, sl 1, k18 (20).

Row 6 Purl.

Row 7 (WS) P4 (4), sl 1 with yarn in back, turn, bring yarn to back, sl 1, k4 (4).

Row 8 P7 (8), sl 1 wyb, turn, bring yarn to back, sl 1, k7 (8).

Row 9 P11 (12) sts, sl 1 wyb, turn, bring yarn to back, sl 1, k11 (12).

Row 10 P14 (16) sts, sl 1 wyb, turn, bring yarn to back, sl 1, k14 (16).

Skeppsta Diamond Pane Pullover continued

Row 11 P17 (19) sts, sl 1 wyb, turn, bring yarn to back, sl 1, p18 (20).

Row 12 Knit.

Rep Rows 1–12 5 times. Then work Rows 1–6 again. Bind off.

▪ Panel B (make 2)

Cast on 18 (20) sts. Knit 1 row. Purl 1 row.

Row 1 (WS) P4 (4), sl 1 wyb, turn, bring yarn to back, sl 1, k4 (4).

Row 2 P7 (8) sts, sl 1 wyb, turn, bring yarn to back, sl 1, k7 (8).

Row 3 P11 (12) sts, sl 1 wyb, turn, bring yarn to back, sl 1, k11 (12).

Row 4 P14 (16) sts, sl 1 wyb, turn, bring yarn to back, sl 1, k14 (16).

Row 5 P17 (19) sts, sl 1 wyb, turn, bring yarn to back, sl 1, p18 (20).

Row 6 Knit.

Row 7 (RS) K4 (4), sl 1 wyf, turn, bring yarn to front, sl 1, p4 (4).

Row 8 K7 (8), sl 1 wyf, turn, bring yarn to front, sl 1, p7 (8).

Row 9 K11 (12), sl 1 wyf, turn, bring yarn to front, sl 1, p11 (12).

Row 10 K14 (16), sl 1 wyf, turn, bring yarn to front, sl 1, p14 (16).

Row 11 K17 (19), sl 1 wyf, turn, bring yarn to front, sl 1, k18 (20).

Row 12 Purl.

Rep Rows 1–12 5 times. Then work Rows 1–6 again. Bind off.

FRONT

Work Panel A twice. Work Panel B twice.

SLEEVES (all sizes)

Cast on 30 (34) sts. Knit 1 row. Purl 2 rows. Change to St st, starting with a knit row. Inc 1 st at each side every 4"/10cm 3 times. When piece measures 16 (17)"/41 (43)cm, bind off all sts.

FINISHING

Join right side of one Panel A to left side of one Panel B. Repeat 4 times, joining together other panels in same way (8 separate pieces are now 4).

▪ Middle Front and Middle Back Seam

Join right sides of Panel B to left sides of Panel A (4 separate pieces are now 2). Join bind-off sts of outside panel for shoulder.

▪ Collar

With circular needle, pick up (56) 64 sts around neck opening. Work St st for 2½"/6cm (all sizes). Work 2 purl rounds. Bind off over next round.

Fit top of sleeve to shoulder edge and join. Join sleeve and side seams. ▪

Danbyholm Pullover

Changing balls of yarn several times across the row in the long ribbed sections of this sweater creates vertical striping in addition to the horizontal striping. Worked in *Kureyon*, this pullover is fun to knit and wear.

Sizes
XS (S, M, L)

Finished Measurements
▓ Chest Approx 32 (36, 40, 44)"/81 (91.5, 101.5, 112)cm
▓ Length Approx 23 (23½, 24, 24½)"/58.5 (60, 61, 62.5)cm

Yarn
Approx 450 (500, 550, 600)g *Kureyon* #134

Needles
One pair each size 8 and 9 (5 and 6mm) straight needles *or size to obtain gauge*

Gauges
15 sts/22 rows = 4"/10cm square with size 9 (6mm) needles in St st
19 sts/24 rows = 4"/10cm square with size 8 (5mm) needles in Rib st

RIB STITCH
Row 1 (RS) K2, *p2, k2, rep from *.
Row 2 (WS) P2, *k2, p2, rep from *.
Rep these 2 rows.

BACK
With size 8 (5mm) needles and using 5 different ends of yarn (both ends of 2 skeins plus one end from a 3rd skein), cast on 14 (16, 18, 20) sts with one end, 14 (16, 18, 20) sts with one end, 14 (16, 18, 20) sts with one end, 14 (16, 18, 20) sts with one end, and 14 (16, 18, 20) sts with one end—70 (80, 90, 100) sts.

Next row (RS) Work across row in Rib st, twisting ends every 14 (16, 18, 20) sts. Work in Rib st until piece measures 10"/25cm, ending with a WS row.

Next row (RS) Changing to size 9 (6 mm) needles and St st, knit across row using yarn from the first rib panel, dec 8 (10, 14, 16) sts evenly across row (knit tog approx every 6th

Danbyholm Pullover continued

and 7th st)—62 (70, 76, 84) sts. Work evenly until piece measures 16"/41cm.

▦ Armhole
Next row (RS) Bind off 3 sts at beg of next 2 rows, then 2 sts at beg of next 2 rows (all sizes)—52 (60, 66, 74) sts. Work evenly until piece measures 22¾ (23¼, 23¾, 24¼)"/58 (59, 60, 61)cm.

▦ Back Neck
Next row (RS) K 17 (20, 23, 26) sts, bind off middle 18 (20, 20, 22) sts, k to end. Work back to neck edge. Bind off 2 (2, 2, 2) sts at neck edge, work to end. Work 1 row. Bind off.

Work other side of neck the same way, reversing the shaping.

FRONT
Cast on and work as for back until piece measures 46cm (all sizes).

▦ Left Side of Front Neck
Next row (RS) K23 (27, 30, 34) sts, k2tog tbl, k1. Turn and work each side of front neck separately. Dec 1 st as described above at neck edge every other row, 10 (11, 11, 12) times—15 (18, 21, 24) sts.

▦ Right Side of Front Neck
Reattach yarn from RS at neck opening. K1,

k2tog, work to end. Dec 1 st as described at neck edge every other row, 10 (11, 11, 12) times—15 (18, 21, 24) sts. Work evenly until piece measures same as for back. Bind off.

SLEEVES
Using one skein of yarn, cast on 38 (42, 42, 46) sts and work in Rib st. for 10"/25cm. *At same time:* Inc 1 st at each side every 8 rows 9 (9, 9, 9) times—56 (60, 60, 64) sts. Work evenly until piece measures 17½ (18, 18, 18½)"/44.5 (46, 46, 47)cm.

▦ Armhole (All sizes)
Next row (RS) Bind off 3 sts at beg of next 2 rows and then 2 sts at beg of next 6 rows. Dec thereafter 1 st at each end of every RS row 5 times. Purl 1 row.

Next row (RS) Bind off 2 sts at beg of next 4 rows. Bind off rem sts over next row.

FINISHING
Join shoulder seams. Using one skein of yarn and from RS, pick up 42 (44, 44, 46) sts along left front neck edge, 30 (34, 34, 34) sts along back neck and 42 (44, 44, 46) sts along right front neck edge—114 (122, 122, 126) sts. Work in Rib st for 15 cm (all sizes). Bind off.

Join sleeves to body and join sleeve seams and body seams. ▪

Sparreholm Hooded Vest

In this fitted, ribbed vest the shaping is worked between the ribs. The hood and the buttons that run along the front and around the hood add a playful feel to this casual top.

Sizes
S (M, L)

Finished Measurements
■ Bust 28¼ (32½, 37)"/72 (83, 94)cm
■ Length 13 (13¾, 14½)"/33 (35, 37)cm

Yarn
Approx 300 (300, 350)g *Silk Garden* #226

Needles
One pair size 9 (5.5mm) straight needles *or size to obtain gauge*
One 30"/80cm size 9 (5.5mm) circular needle *or size to obtain gauge*

Extras
46 ½"/1cm buttons

Gauge
16 sts/22 rows = 4"/10cm square in St st
Take time to check gauge.

NOTES
■ Bust measurements are taken without stretching. The fabric stretches over the body and produces a close fit.
■ Gauge should be attained while working in St st. The actual Rib st of the garment will then pull the fabric together.

BACK
Cast on 93 (103, 113) sts. Work in Twisted Rib st as follows:

Row 1 (WS) *K3, p2, rep from * across row, ending with k3.

Row 2 P3, knit second st on LH needle from the front leaving on needle, knit first st, then slipping both sts onto RH needle, rep from * across row, ending with k3.

Repeat these 2 rows throughout.

Work ½"/1.5cm evenly, ending with a RS row (all sizes).

First dec row (WS) Work 41 (46, 51) sts, k2tog, work 2 sts, k2tog, work 2 sts, k2tog, work to end—90 (100, 110) sts. Work 3 rows.

Second dec row (WS) Work 36 (41, 46) sts, k2tog, work 14 sts, k2tog, work to end—88 (98, 108) sts. Work 3 rows.

Third dec row (WS) Work 31 (36, 41) sts, k2tog, work 22 sts, k2tog, work to end—86 (96, 106) sts. Work 3 rows.

Fourth dec row (WS) Work 26 (31, 36) sts, k2tog, work 30 sts, k2tog, work to end—84 (94, 104) sts. Work 3 rows.

Fifth dec row (WS) Work 21 (26, 31) sts, k2tog, work 38 sts, k2tog, work to end—82 (92, 102) sts. Work 3 rows.

Sixth dec row (WS) Work 16 (21, 26) sts, k2tog, work 46 sts, k2tog, work to end—80 (90, 100) sts. Work 3 rows.

Seventh dec row (WS) Work 11 (16, 21) sts, k2tog, work 54 sts, k2tog, work to end—78 (88, 98) sts. Work 3 rows.

Eighth dec row (WS) Work 6 (11, 16) sts, k2tog, work 62 sts, k2tog, work to end—76 (86, 96) sts. Work 3 rows.

Ninth dec row (WS) Work 1 st, k2tog, work until 3 sts rem, k2tog, work to end—74 (84, 94) sts. Work 3 rows.

Work evenly until piece measures 17 (17, 17)"/43 (43, 43)cm.

▦ Armhole

Bind off from each armhole edge, 4 sts once, 2 sts once and 1 st 3 times (all sizes)—56 (66, 76) sts. Cont to work evenly until armhole

measures 7 (7½, 8)"/18 (19, 20)cm ending with a WS row.

▦ Shoulder Shaping

Bind off at each shoulder edge, 5 (7, 9) sts twice and 4 (5, 6) sts once. Finish row. Place the rem 28 (28, 28) sts on a holder.

FRONT

Cast on 93 (103, 113) sts. Work in Twisted Rib st as follows:

Row 1 (WS) [k3, p2] 9 times, k3, [p2, k3] 9 times.

Row 2 [P3, k second st on LH needle from the front leaving on needle, k first st, then slip both sts onto RH needle] 9 times, p3, [knit second st on left-hand needle from the front, leaving on needle, knit first st, then take both sts onto RH needle, p3] 9 times.

Repeat these 2 rows throughout.

Work ½"/1.5cm evenly, ending with a WS row (all sizes).

First dec row (WS) Work 41 (46, 51) sts, k2tog, work 5 sts, k2tog, work to end—91 (101, 111) sts. (**Note** When viewed from the RS, there are 3 purl sts in the middle of Front.) Work 3 rows.

Second dec row (WS) Work 36 (41, 46) sts, k2tog, work 15 sts, k2tog, work to end—89 (99, 109) sts. Work 3 rows.

Third dec row (WS) Work 31 (36, 41) sts,

Sparreholm Hooded Vest continued

k2tog, work 23 sts, k2tog, work to end—87 (97, 107) sts. Work 3 rows.

Fourth dec row (WS) Work 26 (31, 36) sts, k2tog, work 31 sts, k2tog, work to end—85 (95, 105) sts. Work 3 rows.

Fifth dec row (WS) Work 21 (26, 31) sts, k2tog, work 39 sts, k2tog, work to end—83 (93, 103) sts. Work 3 rows.

Sixth dec row (WS) Work 16 (21, 26) sts, k2tog, work 47 sts, k2tog, work to end—81 (91, 101) sts. Work 3 rows.

Seventh dec row (WS) Work 11 (16, 21) sts, k2tog, work 55 sts, k2tog, work to end—79 (89, 99) sts. Work 3 rows.

Eighth dec row (WS) Work 6 (11, 16) sts, k2tog, work 63 sts, k2tog, work to end—77 (87, 97) sts. Work 3 rows.

Ninth dec row (WS) Work 1 st, k2tog, work until 3 sts rem, k2tog, work to end—75 (85, 95) sts. Work 3 rows.

Work evenly until piece measures 13¾ (13¾, 13¾)"/35 (35, 35)cm (all sizes), ending with a RS row.

▓ Right Side of Neck Opening
Next row (WS) Work 42 (47, 52) sts, turn and work to end. Work only these 42 (47, 52) sts until piece measures 17 (17, 17)"/43 (43, 43)cm.

▒ Armhole

Bind off at armhole edge, 4 sts once, 2 sts once and 1 st 3 times (all sizes). Cont to work evenly until armhole measures 7 (7½, 8)"/18 (19, 20)cm.

▒ Shoulder Shaping

Bind off at shoulder edge, 5 (7, 9) sts twice and 4 (5, 6) sts once. Work to end. Place the rem sts on a holder.

▒ Left Side Neck Opening

With new yarn, cast on 9 (9, 9) sts and from WS, work sts from left side of front neck opening.

Next row (RS) Work sts as established till the cast-on sts rem, then p1, knit second st on LH needle from the front, leaving on needle, knit first st, then, taking both sts onto RH needle, p3, knit second st on LH needle from the front, leaving on needle, knit first st, then, taking both sts onto RH needle, p 1 st. Work evenly until piece measures 17 (17, 17)"/43 (43, 43)cm.

▒ Armhole

Bind off from armhole edge, 4 sts once, 2 sts once and 1 st 3 times. Cont to work evenly over these 42 (47, 52) sts until armhole measures 7 (7½, 8)"/18 (19, 20)cm.

▒ Shoulder Shaping

Bind off at shoulder edge, 5 (7, 9) sts twice and 4 (5, 6) sts once. Place the rem sts on a holder.

HOOD (all sizes)

From RS, transfer sts to a circular needle starting with 19 sts from right side of Front neck opening, then 28 sts across Back neck, and then 19 sts from left side of Front neck opening—66 sts. Work these sts starting from WS for 2 rows.

Next row Work 9 sts, inc 1 st every 4 sts, 13 times (between each twisted rib) until 9 sts rem. Work last 9 sts without inc—79 sts. Work evenly until hood is 2"/5cm.

Next row Work 11 sts, inc 1 st every 5 sts, 13 times (between each twisted rib) until 11 sts rem—92 sts. Work evenly until hood measures approx 12"/30cm. Bind off.

FINISHING

Join shoulder seams. Join side seams. Join seam at top of hood. Place left side of Front neck opening under right side and sew in place with invisible sts. Sew buttons on middle front and around hood edge approx 7 rows apart. ■

Rikissa Panel Cardigan

Like the Skeppsta Pullover (see page 123), this boxy cardigan is constructed of short-row panels short-rows. The panels are knit in *Iro;* the surrounding borders are worked in *Silk Mountain.*

Sizes
S/M (L)

Finished Measurements
▓ Bust 43 (48)"/109 (122)cm
▓ Length 28 (29)"/71 (74)cm

Yarn
200 (200)g *Iro* #69
650 (750)g *Silk Mountain* #13

Needles
One pair size 10½ (7mm) straight needles *or size to obtain gauge*
One 30"/80cm size 10½ (7mm) circular needle *or size to obtain gauge*

Gauge
12 sts/24 rows = 4"/10cm with *Silk Mountain* in Gst
12 sts/18 rows = 4"/10cm with *Iro* in St st

NOTE
If you have trouble locating *Silk Mountain,* you can substitute *Furisode* or another color of *Iro* using the same amount of yarn and size needles.

PANEL A (same for both sizes)
▓ Right Side (make 2)
With *Iro,* cast on 20 sts. Purl 1 row.
Row 1 (RS) *K4, turn, sl 1 st with yarn in front of work, p3.
Row 2 K8, turn, sl 1 st wyf, p7.
Row 3 K12, turn, sl 1 st wyf, p11.
Row 4 K16, turn, sl 1 st wyf, p15.
Row 5 K20, turn, sl 1 st wyf, p19.
Change to *Silk Mountain* and work 4 rows in Gst.
Change to *Iro* and knit 1 row.
Row 11 P4, turn sl 1 st with yarn in back of work, k3.
Row 12 P8, turn sl 1 st wyb, k7.
Row 13 P12, turn sl 1 st wyb, k11.

Rikissa Panel Cardigan continued

Row 14 P16, turn sl 1 st wyb, k15.

Row 15 P20.

Change to *Silk Mountain* and work 4 rows in Gst. *

Repeat between * * for 51"/130cm, ending with Row 5.

Bind off all sts.

Fold the panel and place a marker at the middle fold (the shortest side is toward the sleeve or outside edge).

Place 1 marker 9"/23cm down from the middle on both front and back along the outside edge to mark the armhole.

PANEL B (same for both sizes)
▨ Right Side (make 2)

With *Iro*, cast on 20 sts.

*Knit 1 row.

Row 1 (WS) P4, turn, sl 1 st wyb, k3.

Row 2 P8, turn, sl 1 st wyb, k7.

Row 3 P12, turn, sl 1 st wyb, k11.

Row 4 P16, turn, sl 1 st wyb, k15.

Row 5 P20.

Change to *Silk Mountain* and work 4 rows in Gst.

Change to *Iro*.

Row 11 K4, turn sl 1 st wyf, p3.

Row 12 K8, turn sl 1 st wyf, p7.

Row 13 K12, turn sl 1 st wyf, p11.

Row 14 K16, turn sl 1 st wyf, p15.

Row 15 K20, turn sl 1 st wyf, p19.

Change to *Silk Mountain* and work 4 rows in Gst. *

Repeat between * *, 12 more times.

Work Rows 1–5. Bind off all sts.

Fold the panel and place a marker at the middle fold (the shortest side is toward the sleeve or outside edge).

Place 1 marker 9"/23cm down from the middle on both front and back along the outside edge to mark the armhole.

SLEEVES (make 2)

With *Silk Mountain*, cast on 56 sts and work in Gst. Dec 1 st at each side every 8 rows, 12 times—32 sts. Work until piece measures 19"/48cm. Bind off all sts.

MIDDLE BACK PANEL

With *Silk Mountain*, cast on 16 (20) sts and work in Gst for 24"/61cm (both sizes). Piece should be ½"/1cm shorter than to middle marker. Bind off all sts.

Place the Middle Back Panel between Panel A and Panel B with the long side of the panels at inside. Join.

EDGING AROUND BACK

Starting from the Left armhole, with RS facing and with *Silk Mountain*, pick up 50 sts along the Left side, 1 st in corner, 18 sts across Left Panel, 14 sts across Middle Back Panel, 18 sts across Right Panel, 1 st in corner, 50 sts along Right side to armhole. Knit 1 row, placing a marker at each side of corner sts.

▓ Size S/M

Row 1 (RS) K50, inc 1 st, k1, inc 1 st, k50, inc 1 st, k1, inc 1 st, k50.

Rows 2, 4, 6, 8, 10 and 12 Knit.

Row 3 K51, inc 1 st, k1, inc 1 st, k52, inc 1 st, k1, inc 1 st, k51.

Rows 5, 7, 9 and 11 Continue with the incs on each side of the corner st as for Row 3.

Row 13 Bind off all sts.

▓ Size M/L

Row 1 (RS) K50, inc 1 st, k1, inc 1 st, k50, inc 1 st, k1, inc 1 st, k50.

Rows 2, 4, 6, 8, 10,12, 14, 16 and 18 Knit.

Row 3 K51, inc 1 st, k1, inc 1 st, k52, inc 1 st, k1, inc 1 st, k51.

Rows 5, 7, 9,11, 13, 15 and 17 Continue with the incs on each side of the corner st as for Row 3.

Row 19 Bind off all sts.

EDGING AROUND RIGHT FRONT

Starting from the Left armhole, with RS facing and with *Silk Mountain*, pick up 50 sts along the Left side, 1 st in corner, 18 sts, 1 st in corner, 80 sts along Middle Front edge, then cast on 14 (16) new sts at end of row. Knit 1 row, placing a marker at each side of corner sts.

野呂 137

Rikissa Panel Cardigan continued

▦ Size S/M
Row 1 (RS) K50, inc 1 st, k1, inc 1 st, k18, inc 1 st, k1, inc 1 st, k94.

Rows 2, 4, 6, 8, 10 and 12 Knit.

Row 3 K51, inc 1 st, k1, inc 1 st, k20, inc 1 st, k1, inc 1 st, k95.

Rows 5, 7, 9 and 11 Continue with the incs on each side of the corner st as for Row 3.

Row 13 Bind off all sts.

▦ Size M/L
Row 1 (RS) K50, inc 1 st, k1, inc 1 st, k18, inc 1 st, k1, inc 1 st, k94.

Rows 2, 4, 6, 8, 10, 12, 14, 16 and 18 Knit.

Row 3 K51, inc 1 st, k1, inc 1 st, k20, inc 1 st, k1, inc 1 st, k95.

Rows 5, 7, 9, 11, 13, 15 and 17 Continue with the incs on each side of the corner st as for Row 3.

Row 19 Bind off all sts.

▦ Size S/M
Row 1 (RS) K94, inc 1 st, k1, inc 1 st, k18, inc 1 st, k1, inc 1 st, k50.

Rows 2, 4, 6, 8, 10 and 12 Knit.

Row 3 K95, inc 1 st, k1, inc 1 st, k20, inc 1 st, k1, inc 1 st, k51.

Rows 5, 7, 9 and 11 Continue with the incs on each side of the corner st as for Row 3.

Row 13 Bind off all sts.

▦ Size M/L
Row 1 (RS) K94, inc 1 st, k1, inc 1 st, k18, inc 1 st, k1, inc 1 st, k50.

Rows 2, 4, 6, 8, 10, 12, 14, 16 and 18 Knit.

Row 3 K95, inc 1 st, k1, inc 1 st, k20, inc 1 st, k1, inc 1 st, k51.

Rows 5, 7, 9, 11, 13, 15, 17 Continue with the incs on each side of the corner st as for Row 3.

Row 19 Bind off all sts.

EDGING AROUND LEFT FRONT

With *Silk Mountain*, cast on 14 (16) sts, cont down the Middle Front edge picking up 80 sts, 1 st in corner, 18 sts, 1 st in corner, 50 sts along outside edge to armhole. Place a marker at each side of corner sts.

FINISHING

Join seam at back neck. Join collar to back neck. Fit sleeves into armholes and join. Join sleeve seams and side seams, leaving 4"/10cm openings at bottom sides. ■

Stallarholmen Throw

This afghan is constructed of squares within squares in *Kureyon*. The squares are joined to make a rectangle and then bordered with *Cash Iroha*. The striping of the yarns is put to good use creating a kind of patchwork effect.

Finished Measurements
47" x 63"/120cm x 160cm

Yarn
Approx 1100g *Kureyon* #92
Approx 50g *Cash Iroha* #22

Needles
One pair size 8 (5mm) straight needles
or size to obtain gauge
One 30"/80cm size 8 (5mm) circular needle
or size to obtain gauge

Gauge
16 sts/24 rows = 4"/10cm over St st
16 sts/32 rows = 4"/10cm over Gst
Take time to check gauge.

NOTE
Each block is comprises of 3 concentric squares—A, B and C (or AA, BB and CC)— and is worked from the outside inward, binding off at inside of squares A and B (AA and BB) to form an opening for the next square. It is important that the outer measurements of all squares are correct to ensure symmetry. To avoid having to measure every square in progress, I found it helpful to note the number of rows worked for each square and, instead, count the rows while knitting. Remember that there is a difference in the row gauge between St st squares and Gst squares.

A, B, C Blocks (make 6)
■ **Square A—Gst** (16 x 16"/40 x 40cm)
Cast on 64 sts and work 3¼"/8cm.
Bind-off row (RS) (Work each side of square separately.) K13, bind off 38 sts, k13. Turn. Work these last 13 sts for 9½"/24cm, ending with a WS row. Break yarn. Reattach yarn from WS to inside edge of first 13 sts and work for 9½"/24cm, ending with a WS row.

Cast-on row (RS) k13, cast on 38 sts, k13 (from left side of square). Work over all sts for 3¼"/8cm. Bind off.

▨ **Square B—St st** (9½ x 9½"/24 x 24cm) With RS facing, pick up 38 sts evenly along right *inside* edge of Square A and work for 3¼"/8cm.

Bind-off row (RS) (Work each side of square separately). K13, bind off 12 sts, k13. Turn. Work these last 13 sts for 3¼"/8cm, ending with a WS row. Break yarn. Reattach yarn from WS and work first 13 sts for 3¼"/8cm, ending with a WS row.

Cast-on row (RS) K13, cast on 12 sts, k13 (from left side of square). Work over all sts for 3¼"/8cm. Bind off.

▨ **Square C—Gst** (3¼ x 3¼"/8cm x 8cm) With RS facing, pick up 13 sts evenly along

Assembly Diagram

A	AA	A
AA	A	AA
A	AA	A
AA	A	AA

Variation: Baby Blanket

You can also use this pattern to knit a baby blanket. You'll need approx 400g *Kureyon* #92 and 50g *Cash Iroha* #22 and the same needles as for the throw. Work 2 blocks with A, B, C squares and 2 blocks with AA, BB, CC squares. To finish, lay out the 4 blocks in a square. Join blocks. For the border, using Cash Iroha and circular needle (RS facing), pick up 128 sts along outside edge and work 4 rows in Gst. Bind off all sts. Work border on rem edges as described. The finished measurements are 31½ x 31½"/80 x 80cm.

right *inside* edge of Square B and work 3¼"/8cm. Bind off.

AA, BB, CC Blocks (make 6)
▦ **Square AA—St st** (16 x 16"/40 x 40cm)
Work as for Square A, but using St st.

▦ **Square BB—Gst** (9½ x 9½"/24 x 24cm)
Work as for Square B, but using Gst.

▦ **Square CC—St st** (3¼ x 3¼"/8cm x 8cm)
Work as for Square C, but using St st.

FINISHING OF BLOCKS
Baste or pin squares into place and join the outside edge of Square B (BB) to inside edge of Square A (AA). Then join outside edge of Square C (CC) to inside edge of Square B (BB). Steam-block under a damp dishtowel to correct size.

FINISHING OF THROW
Lay out all 12 blocks according to diagram. Join blocks.

▦ **Border**
Using *Cash Iroha* and circular needle (RS facing), pick up approx 192 sts along one short edge of throw. Work 4 rows in Gst. Bind off all sts. Pick up approx 256 sts along one long edge of throw. Work 4 rows in Gst. Bind off all sts. Work border on rem edges as described. ▪

野呂　143

Yarns Used in This Book

BLOSSOM

Fiber content: 40% wool, 30% kid mohair, 20% silk, 10% nylon

Yardage (per ball): 77yd/70m

Weight (per ball): 1½oz/40g

Gauge: 14 sts and 20 rows over 4"/10cm using size 7/4.5mm needles

Yarn weight: 5

CASH IROHA

Fiber content: 40% silk, 30% lambswool, 20% cashmere, 10% nylon

Yardage (per ball): 100yd/91m

Weight (per ball): 1½oz/40g

Gauge: 20 sts and 26 rows over 4"/10cm using size 7/4.5mm needles

Yarn weight: 4

CASHMERE ISLAND

Fiber content: 60% wool, 30% cashmere, 10% nylon

Yardage (per ball): 110yd/100m

Weight (per ball): 1½oz/40g

Gauge: 22 sts and 28 rows over 4"/10cm using size 6/4mm needles

Yarn weight: 3

HANNA SILK

Fiber content: 100% silk

Yardage (per ball): 132yd/120m

Weight (per ball): 1¾oz/50g

Gauge: 16 sts and 20 rows over 4"/10cm using size 8/5mm needles

Yarn weight: 4

IRO

Fiber content: 75% wool, 25% silk

Yardage (per ball): 132yd/120m

Weight (per ball): 3½oz/100g

Gauge: 12 sts and 16 rows over 4"/10cm using size 11/8mm needles

Yarn weight: 5

KOCHORAN

Fiber content: 50% wool, 30% angora, 20% silk

Yardage (per ball): 176yd/161m

Weight (per ball): 3½oz/100g

Gauge: 14 sts and 20 rows over 4"/10cm using size 10½/6.5mm needles

Yarn weight: 5

KUREYON

Fiber content: 100% wool

Yardage (per ball): 110yd/100m

Weight (per ball): 1¾oz/50g

Gauge: 18 sts and 24 rows over 4"/10cm using size 7/4.5mm needles

Yarn weight: 4

NIJI

Fiber content: 45% wool, 25% silk, 25% kid mohair, 5% nylon

Yardage (per ball): 97yd/88m

Weight (per ball): 1½oz/40g

Gauge: 18 sts and 24 rows over 4"/10cm using size 7/4.5mm needles

Yarn weight: 4

NOTE Noro is constantly developing new yarns. Some of the yarns used in the original patterns may no longer be available. Substitute yarns have been suggested in the patterns where necessary. Because of the nature of Noro yarns, the results will vary. If you are using substituting yarns, it is especially important to check your gauge.

1   2   3   4

5   6   7   8

9   10   11   12

13   14

1 Blossom   2 Cash Iroha   3 Cashmere Island
4 Hanna Silk   5 Iro   6 Kochoran   7 Kureyon
8 Niji   9 Silk Garden   10 Silk Garden Chunky
11 Silk Garden Lite   12 Silk Mountain
13 Silver Thaw   14 Transitions

Yarns continued

▦ SILK GARDEN

Fiber content: 45% silk, 45% mohair, 10% lambswool

Yardage (per ball): 122yd/112m

Weight (per ball): 1¾oz/50g

Gauge: 18 sts and 24 rows over 4"/10cm using size 7/4.5mm needles

Yarn weight: 4

▦ SILK GARDEN LITE

Fiber content: 45% silk, 45% mohair, 10% lambswool

Yardage (per ball): 137yd/125m

Weight (per ball): 1¾oz/50g

Gauge: 22 sts and 28 rows over 4"/10cm using size 6/4mm needles

Yarn weight: 3

▦ SILVER THAW

Fiber content: 50% wool, 25% super angora, 25% polyamide

Yardage (per ball): 242yd/220m

Weight (per ball): 3½oz/100g

Gauge: 18 sts and 24 rows over 4"/10cm using size 8/5mm needles

Yarn weight: 4

▦ SILK GARDEN CHUNKY

Fiber content: 45% silk, 45% mohair, 10% lambswool

Yardage (per ball): 66yd/60m

Weight (per ball): 1¾oz/50g

Gauge: 14 sts and 20 rows over 4"/10cm using size 11/8mm needles

Yarn weight: 5

▦ SILK MOUNTAIN

Fiber content: 65% wool, 25% silk, 10% kid mohair

Yardage (per ball): 55yd/50m

Weight (per ball): 1¾oz/50g

Gauge: 14 sts and 19 rows over 4"/10cm using size 10/6mm needles

Yarn weight: 5

▦ TRANSITIONS

Fiber content: 55% wool, 10% silk, 7% kid mohair, 7% cashmere, 7% angora, 7% camel, 7% alpaca

Yardage (per ball): 132yd/120m

Weight (per ball): 3½oz/100g

Gauge: 14 sts and 19 rows over 4"/10cm using size 10/6mm needles

Yarn weight: 5

These yarns are suggested as possible substitutes for some of the yarns used in the patterns.

▦ CHIRIMEN

Fiber content: 60% cotton, 24% silk, 16% wool

Yardage (per ball): 114yd/104m

Weight (per ball): 1¾oz/50g

Gauge: 22 sts and 28 rows over 4"/10cm using size 6/4mm needles

Yarn weight: 3

▦ FURISODE

Fiber content: 45% silk, 40% cotton, 15% wool

Yardage (per ball): 241yd/220m

Weight (per ball): 3½oz/100g

Gauge: 14 sts and 20 rows over 4"/10cm using size 9 or 10/5.5 or 6mm needles

Yarn weight: 5

▦ TAIYO

Fiber content: 40% cotton, 30% silk, 15% wool, 15% nylon

Yardage (per ball): 220yd/201m

Weight (per ball): 3½oz/100g

Gauge: 18 sts and 24 rows over 4"/10cm using size 7 or 8/4.5 or 5mm needles

Yarn weight: 4

Worldwide Distributors

To locate retailers of Noro yarns, contact one of the following distributors:

AUSTRALIA/NEW ZEALAND
Prestige Yarns Pty Ltd
P.O Box 39
Bulli NSW 2516
T: +61 02 4285 6669
info@prestigeyarns.com
www.prestigeyarns.com

BELGIUM/HOLLAND
Pavan
Thomas Van Theemsche
Meerlaanstraat 73
9860 Balegem (Oostrezele)
T: +32 (0) 9 221 85 94
pavan@pandora.be

CANADA
Diamond Yarns Ltd
155 Martin Ross Avenue
Unit 3
Toronto, Ontario M3J 2L9
T: 001 416 736 6111
F: 001 416 736 6112
www.diamondyarns.com

DENMARK
Fancy Knit
Hovedvejen 71
8586 Oerum Djurs
Ramten
T: (45) 59 4621 89
roenneburg@mail.dk

FINLAND
Priima
Hameentie 26
00530 Helsinki
T: +358 (0) 9 7318 0010
maria.hellbom@priima.net
www.duodesign.fi

FRANCE
Laines Plassard
La Filature
71800 Varennes-sous-Dun
T: +33 (0)3 85282828
F: +33 (0) 85282829
info@laines-plassard.com

GERMANY/AUSTRIA/ SWITZERLAND/ LUXEMBOURG
Designer Yarns (Deutschland) Ltd
Sachsstrasse 30
D-50259 Pulheim-Brauweiler
Germany
T: +49 (0) 2234 205453
F: +49 (0) 2234 205456
kk@designeryarns.de

JAPAN
Eisaku & Co Ltd
55 Shimoda Ohibino Azaichou
Ichinomiya Aichi
491 01505
T: +81 586 51 3113
F: +81 586 51 2625
noro@io.ocn.ne.jp
www.eisakunoro.com

SPAIN
Oyambre Needlework SL
Balmes, 200 At. 4
08006 Barcelona
T: +34 (0) 93 487 26 72
F: +34 (0) 93 218 6694
info@oyambreonline.com

SWEDEN
Hamilton Yarns
Storgatan 14
64730 Mariefred
T: +46 (0) 159 12006
www.hamiltondesign.biz

UK & EUROPE
Designer Yarns Ltd
Units 8–10
Newbridge Industrial Estate
Pitt Street
Keighley BD21 4 PQ
T: +44 (0)1535 664222
F: +44 (0)1535 664333
alex@designeryarns.uk.com
www.designeryarns.uk.com

USA
Knitting Fever Inc.
315 Bayview Avenue
Amityville, NY 11701
T: 516 546 3600
F: 516 546 6871
www.knittingfever.com

野呂 147

Abbreviations

approx	approximately	patt	pattern	WS	wrong (back) side of work
beg	beginning	pfb	purl in front and back of st	wyb	with yarn in back
CC	contrasting color	psso	pass slipped st over	wyf	with yarn in front
cont	continue	p2tog	purl two sts together	yo	yarn over; work by placing the yarn over the right-hand needle
dc	double crochet	p-wise	purlwise		
dec	decrease	rem	remaining		
dp	double point	rep	repeat		
foll	following	RH	right-hand		
g	gram(s)	rnd(s)	round(s)		
Gst	garter stitch	RS	right (front) side of work		
inc	increase				
k	knit	sc	single crochet		
kfb	knit in front and back of stitch	skpo	slip 1, knit 1, pass slipped st over knit stitch		
k2tog	knit two sts together				
LH	left-hand	sl	slip 1 st purlwise unless otherwise indicated		
m	meter(s)				
mm	millimeter(s)	st(s)	stitch(es)		
m1	make one stitch by placing a backward loop onto the right-hand needle	St st	stockinette stitch		
		tbl	through back loop		
p	purl	tog	together		

Skill Levels

◼◻◻◻
Beginner Ideal first project.

◼◼◻◻
Easy Basic stitches, minimal shaping and simple finishing.

◼◼◼◻
Intermediate For knitters with some experience. More intricate stitches, shaping and finishing.

◼◼◼◼
Experienced For knitters able to work patterns with complicated shaping and finishing.

 The lovely characters shown throughout this book mean "Noro" in Japanese.

Dedications

To the Lord Jesus Christ, in whose name all my prayers are made, heard, and answered.

To my mother, Karolyn A. Mitchell, who taught me to have hope and to believe, and through her prayers I have come to know the Lord and his Divine Art.

—M.W.

My gratitude to Michele Wood for her ennobling artistic vision; Kazumi and Kenji, my children, for nurturing my soul; and special thanks to my grandmother, Rev. Viola A. Gibson, for inspiring knowledge, faith, and cultural connection. Bless her heart.

—T. I.

Gospel Means GOOD NEWS!

When the artist, Michele Wood, and I worked together on *I See the Rhythm,* about the history of African-American music, we both felt there was so much more to explore in one musical form in particular: gospel music.

Gospel evolved from the early African-American spiritual, but no one can say exactly when and where the spiritual got its start. Did enslaved Africans copy and change the European Christian and folk music? How many African slaves were exposed to Christianity before they were brought to the Americas? Did those slaves bring their own African religious songs to the New World and modify them? Did slaves create their own unique songs? Historians are still asking these questions.

What we do know is that the African-American spiritual was born out of the brutality of slavery and evolved into what we know today as "gospel music." It is a response to the centuries of injustice and discrimination endured by enslaved Africans.

In this book, Michele and I want to take you on a trip through time to learn more about African-American history and gospel music. We want you to see through Michele's pictures and my words how the lives of African Americans— and our spirit—influenced the music and how the music influenced our lives. How gospel music expressed our pain and sorrows, uplifted our souls, and gave us the strength to endure and survive.

The good news is that African Americans and our unique culture have not only survived, we've thrived! And the good news is gospel.

Toyomi Igus

The themes of African-American gospel songs are often drawn from Bible stories. This picture is an illustration of the prophetess Miriam leading Hebrew women in song and dance, celebrating the Exodus of the Hebrew slaves and the defeat of the Egyptians. Gospel music also reflects the natural world and personal experiences of African Americans.

P.S. Remember Missy in *I See the Rhythm?* She is the spirit of the artist, Michele Wood, who appears as a little girl in each painting. Look closely at the pictures and see if you can find her!

1485: The Portuguese colonize the islands in the Gulf of Guinea to make sugar. But they need slaves to work the tropical plantations. This is the beginning of the slave trade; a thousand Africans a year are brought in to work the plantations.

1494: The first Africans arrive with Christopher Columbus to the West Indian island of Hispaniola (today called Haiti). They are free people.

1511: The first Africans who are slaves arrive in Hispaniola.

I see the rhythm.
I see the rhythm of Africa,

the motherland of humanity.

I see the rhythm of my people, land, and spirit in harmony.

The drumbeats from our souls echo the movement of the earth,

the journey of the sun and the mystery of our birth.

We feel the flow of the rivers, the swing of the trees,

the migration of the birds, the tides of the seas.

We dance to the rhythm of our hearts, we sing our songs of strife,

for as creations of the creator, we are connected to all life.

But then … in one moment …

grasping hands, clanking chains,

my voice is muffled, my family slain.

My heart is broken, my faith is shaken.
To what fearful place am I being taken?

I remember the rhyhms of my homeland …

And that rhythm lives on in me.

1522: African slaves rebel in Hispaniola. This is the first slave uprising in the New World.

From 1500–Civil War (1860s): Slaves are brought to the Caribbean Islands, the United States, and South America to provide cheap labor for landowners. About ten million Africans survive the crossing of the Atlantic Ocean, known as the Middle Passage, to the New World.

There are many different peoples, countries, languages, and customs in Africa. The same is true of religions. Africans are Muslim, Christian, Jewish, and some still practice their native worship rituals. For all Africans, music is devotional. In this picture, the first panel shows a woman washing clothes in the river, while African villagers are being captured by European slavers. The dye leaking into the river from the ends of the two red scarves represents the blood shed by African people who died in the slave trade. Many West African tribes had customs similar to baptism, which the water of the river represents. The center panel shows villagers dancing and drumming in celebration. Some tribes believe that the spirits are summoned with the drumming.

Upon arrival in the new land, Africans tried to retain their tribal religious practices, but they lost them over time. They also lost their languages. At first, the enslaved blacks could not communicate well with each other, but eventually they adopted the language of the slave masters. Jesus is shown here as one of the slaves, illustrating how, even though the Bible was used to justify slavery, Jesus suffered on behalf of all mankind. The minister on the right preaches at a plantation revival meeting. These meetings provide comfort to the hard-working slaves. The conversion of slaves to Christianity in the 1700s is called the Great Awakening.

1619: Slavery begins in the United States, when a Dutch ship steals a cargo of enslaved Africans from the Spanish. The ship arrives in Jamestown with "20 negars" to exchange for supplies. These are the first Africans to arrive in the English North American colonies.

1634: Maryland officially adopts slavery, the first American colony of many to do so.

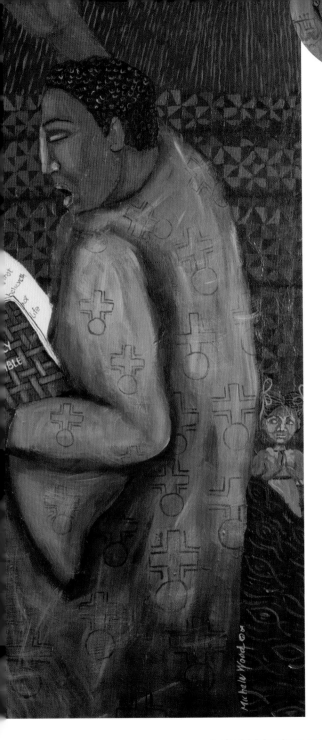

I see the rhythm
of a New World,

strange beliefs,
a life of despair,
a life of grief.

I am a motherless child, lost and confused,
trapped in the dark—used and abused.
In this new land, there are unceasing commands.
But my spirit makes new demands
of hope, home, future, salvation.
FREEDOM *from backbreaking work and strife.*
FREEDOM *to define a new life.*

But the labor beats down my body.
The hate demeans my soul.
Can I reclaim the spirit that they stole?

We find the answer in our music and in our faith
that lightens our plight.
I see the rhythm of the Americas,
as Africa's spirit shines on so bright.

1642: The Fugitive Slave Law is passed in Virginia to punish those who help enslaved people escape. Runaway slaves are branded with an "R" when they are caught.

Late 1600s: Slaves are not allowed to be educated or taught to read—even the Bible. Most Christian colonists were slave owners and discouraged the conversion of slaves to the religion. The Quakers, however, welcomed both slaves and freedmen.

1661: A law in Maryland is passed ensuring that enslaved blacks who convert to Christianity will remain slaves.

1754: Benjamin Banneker, a 21-year-old black man, makes the first clock in colonial America, one of his many inventions.

1758: The first known black church in North America is founded, the African Baptist or "Bluestone" Church in Virgina.

1770: Crispus Attucks, a sailor and an escaped slave, is the first civilian shot when the British attack a protesting crowd in Boston, an event known as the Boston Massacre. Attucks is the first hero of the American Revolution who died for speaking out against English rule.

I see the rhythm of Plantation Sundays.

Shhhhh! Quietly

we walk past the fields
we worked all week
and into the forest just beyond the creek.

Master's going to church and so are we,

but quietly, quietly.

Then we are clear—no one around. Only us to hear.

Mama hums, low and strong. Eyes closed, we hum along.

Feet shuffle, arms wave, and voices lift

our spirits higher and higher.

Quiet no more, we clap our hands, and stomp our feet.

"Glory!" she says and "Glory!" we repeat

and repeatpeatpeat

as our souls fill with song and rise to greet the heavens,

the one place where we belong.

Although slaves were not allowed to form their own churches in the South, they found ways to worship. They would gather in hidden clearings in the woods or in the secret "praise houses" on the plantations on Sundays. Because drums were outlawed, they used their hands and feet to keep time and create the rhythms, dancing in a circle while singing spirituals. This tradition was called the "ring shout."

1775–1781: Americans fight the English for independence. This is the American Revolution. The Declaration of Independence in 1776 establishes the new United States of America. After the American Revolution, 10,000 slaves are freed in the North. But slavery is still going strong in the American South.

1793: Eli Whitney's invention of the cotton gin increases the demand for slave labor.

1793: A federal fugitive slave law calls for the return of slaves who escape across state lines.

1800: Gabriel Prosser, an enslaved blacksmith, organizes a slave revolt in Richmond, Virginia. The conspiracy is uncovered. Prosser and a number of the rebels are hanged. Virginia tightens its slave laws.

1801: The first hymnal for black churches is published, *Collection of Spiritual Songs and Hymns Selected from Various Authors,* by Richard Allen, minister of the first independent black denomination, the African Methodist Episcopal Church.

1808: Congress stops the importation of more slaves from Africa.

1830s: The camp meetings that start the Second Great Awakening are popular. Both blacks and whites flock to these revival meetings, where many are converted to Christianity. Often whites sing with the black slaves.

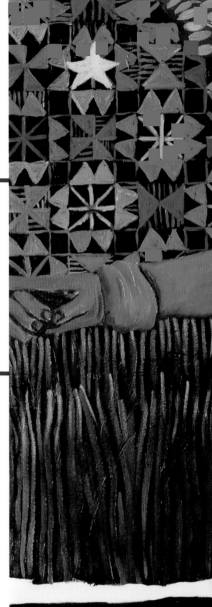

I see the rhythm of
OUR HOPE

for freedom in the Promised Land
on the face of Brother Otis as he takes my sister's hand

and they run.

Swiftly.
Silently.

I see them mouth their good-byes

with tears in their eyes,

slinking past our shacks,

taking one quick look back

to wave at me.

I watch their night shadows as, bodies fueled by fear,

they run through the fields hoping the dogs won't hear

their hearts pounding in their ears

or their feet slapping through the muddy banks of the river.

When they step into the water, my sister gives a shiver.

Brother Otis holds her tighter,
knowing that the river will deliver
them to FREEDOM.

Former slave Harriet Tubman helped other slaves escape through the "Underground Railroad" to freedom in the North, moving secretly from town to town. They were helped along the way by abolitionists, people who opposed slavery. Here, the red and white stripes and maple leaf on her skirt symbolize the flag of Canada. It is believed that Tubman used spirituals as signals to slaves preparing for escape. The spiritual "Wade in the Water" instructed slaves how to throw the slave trackers' bloodhounds off their scent by walking through water.

1831: Nat Turner leads seventy fellow slaves in a two-day rebellion in Virginia, killing sixty whites. The same year, William Lloyd Garrison begins publishing the *Liberator*, a weekly newspaper that calls for the abolition of slavery. Later, former slave Frederick Douglass joins Garrison's antislavery movement.

1840s: People of the northern and southern states become increasingly divided over slavery. The issue also divides religious communities. In 1840, southern Methodists can not agree with northern Methodists about the morality of slavery.

1847: Former slave Frederick Douglass launches his abolitionist newspaper, the *North Star*.

1857: The Dred Scott legal case decides that Congress does not have the right to ban slavery in states and that slaves are not citizens.

1861: The Civil War between the northern and southern states begins.

1863: President Abraham Lincoln issues the Emancipation Proclamation, declaring "that all persons held as slaves" will be free.

In 1865, slavery was abolished in America. This day of liberation is called Day of Jubilee. The image above shows newly freed slaves moving north to freedom and hopeful prosperity. The books in this image represent the opportunities blacks now had for education. The church symbolizes how black churches became safe havens for African Americans as they settled into their new communities.

1865: Congress establishes the Freedmen's Bureau to protect the rights of newly freed blacks. The Civil War ends; President Lincoln is assassinated; and the Ku Klux Klan is formed by ex-Confederates.

1865–1866: The "Black Codes" are passed by southern states. These laws try to drastically restrict the rights of newly freed slaves.

1866–1877: The Reconstruction Era begins. Congress attempts to reorganize the states devastated by the Civil War and establish a non-slave society.

1867: Black colleges like Fisk, Howard University, and Morehouse start to graduate a new generation of black leaders.

I see the rhythm of jubilee day

in the hopeful faces of my family as we make our way
north to find our new home.
Our wagon is packed with food, quilts, our personal things,
not quite sure where we're going or how much to bring,
and to pass the time away, our people hum and sing
our old spirituals.

"We free now, baby," Mama whispers as we bounce and sway
with the wagon's twists and turns over roads of clay
through the land that oppressed us
to a new world, a brand-new day.

Free.

We waited so long to say that word; we thought our prayers would never be heard.
But what is free?
What does that mean?
Am I free to be me?
Will I ever be seen?

Or will their faces always turn mean when we arrive on the scene?
I see the rhythm of our emancipation
in the songs sung by freed men who are still not free.

1867: Fisk University organizes a choir of ex-slaves into the Fisk Jubilee Singers. Groups like this popularize the old African-American spirituals worldwide when they tour and perform.

1868: The Fourteenth Amendment to the Constitution states that individuals born in the United States are American citizens, including those born as slaves.

1870: The Fifteenth Amendment to the Constitution gives blacks the right to vote.

1877: Attempts by the government to provide basic civil rights for blacks quickly erode after Reconstruction ends.

1879–1880: The Black Exodus takes place. Tens of thousands of African Americans migrate from southern states to Kansas to find a better life.

1882–1930: Over 3,700 men and women are reported lynched or hanged. Most are southern blacks. Lynching is a tactic used by southern racists to brutalize and intimidate black people.

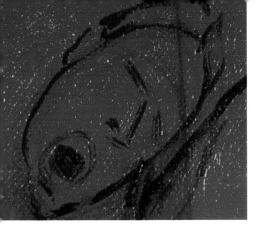

I see the rhythm in the sanctified churches

of black folk who flock to the pews

after days of doing hard jobs white folks don't want to do.

Every Sunday morning, in the California heat,

I follow the grown-ups down to meet

all the friends and neighbors hurrying to get a seat

at Azusa Street.

There I watch as Pastor Seymour preaches and beseeches

us to feel the spirit.

Then, one by one, the grown-ups stand and testify about His commands.

Their bodies shake, their voices lift and shout.

I get a little nervous as I look about and see

the people I know move in some strange dance,

speaking in tongues, falling in a trance...

"Amen!" the preacher yells.

"Amen!" we say.

"Hallelujah!"

"Hallelujah!"

This goes on all day,

until, one by one, they each surrender

to experience some ecstatic splendor

that leaves them refreshed and soft and tender

ready to start a new week.

I see the rhythm at Azusa Street,

when the spirit rises and starts to speak.

1896 : The Supreme Court decision *Plessy v. Ferguson* says that racial segregation is constitutional. This decision allows the Jim Crow laws in the South to take hold. These laws kept blacks oppressed after the Civil War.

1907 : Madame C. J. Walker builds a beauty products empire developing hair care products for black women. She becomes the first African-American millionaire.

1909 : The National Association for the Advancement of Colored People (NAACP) is founded by black and white intellectuals and led by W. E. B. Du Bois. It becomes the most influential black civil rights organization in America, dedicated to political equality and social justice.

1909 : Admiral Robert E. Peary, African-American Matthew Henson, and four Eskimo scouts become the first men to reach the North Pole.

1914 : Marcus Garvey establishes the Universal Negro Improvement Association, an influential black nationalist organization "to promote the spirit of race pride" and create a sense of worldwide unity among blacks.

1917 : The United States joins the Allied Forces in World War I.

To escape the South, African-Americans also migrated west. At 312 Azusa Street, Los Angeles, California, the Pentecostal movement is believed to have been born. In this picture, people at this Azusa Street revival meeting feel "the Spirit" and are encouraged to "testify," that is, speak, sing, and dance spontaneously about their faith. Much of African-American gospel music has its roots in these "sanctified" or Pentecostal churches.

I SEE THE RHYTHM of BRONZEVILLE

on Chicago's South Side,

where black folk come together to create, reside,

and build a community full of love and pride.

FOR A WHILE, WE ARE FINE.

WE LOOK FORWARD TO MORE.

but after Black Tuesday, we become more poor—

Papa loses his job to the man next door—

and Mama has to cook *and* start cleaning floors.

We find escape through our artists, who make jazz and blues so fine—

LOUIS ARMSTRONG. BESSIE SMITH.

ETHEL WATERS. FATHA HINES—

and in our churches, we start to hear the same rhythm lines

when the Father of Gospel makes new music that shines on and on.

"Precious Lord, take my hand," he wrote when she died.
"Precious Lord, take my hand," he sings and we cry.

I see the rhythms of **THOMAS DORSEY** and his choirs

who made music that inspires

all of us who are so, so tired.

Like New York's Harlem Renaissance, Chicago's South Side in the 1920s and '30s was also a center of African-American creativity in an area called "Bronzeville." Thomas Dorsey, known as the Father of Gospel, moved to Chicago to join the exciting blues and jazz scene as a performer. It was while he attended a National Baptist Convention there that he was inspired to create a unique gospel music. He added blues and jazz elements to religious hymns, creating the choral gospel blues. Here, Dorsey leads a gospel chorus at Ebenezer Baptist Church in Chicago.

1921: African-American Bessie Coleman becomes the first woman to receive an international pilot's license to fly.

At the **1921** National Baptist Convention, evangelist W. M. Nix is invited to preach and promote the *Gospel Pearls* hymnal—the first publication by a black congregation to use the term "gospel."

1923: The famous Cotton Club opens in Harlem.

1929: The American stock market crashes on what is known as "Black Tuesday." This triggers the Great Depression, which lasts for more than ten years. During this time, almost one-fourth of the country's workforce is unemployed. The jobs held by African Americans are often taken away and given to whites.

1932: Thomas Dorsey's wife and son die in childbirth. In his grief, he writes "Take My Hand, Precious Lord," one of the world's most popular gospel songs.

I SEE THE RHYTHM OF GOSPEL QUARTETS

in the soulful voices heard on our radio set.

Soul Stirrers, Pilgrim Travelers, Dixie Hummingbirds

record their a cappella harmonies to spread the word

When the Golden Gate Quartet comes to our town,

     of the gospel.

     me and June Bug run around

        trying to find a way to hear their sound.

"Shoo!" says the ticket taker when we try to slide by.

"Get outta here!" says the guard when we sneak in on the sly.

So we climb on up that big sycamore tree,

     and we perch ourselves out on a limb to see

    the Quartet in all their finery.

   For the next hour, me and June Bug, caught up in the stories,

  pretend to be Bible heroes in their tales of glory,

     Joshua and the battle, Jonah and the whale,

      Sampson, Job, and Noah, Ezekiel, and Gabriel.

I see the rhythm of gospel in these happy harmonies

       that never fail.

1939: Because she is black, famous opera singer Marian Anderson is forbidden to perform at Constitution Hall in Washington, D. C., by the Daughters of the Revolution. She instead performs on the steps of the Lincoln Memorial on Easter Day, drawing an audience of 75,000 people.

1941: President Franklin Roosevelt and his wife, Eleanor, invite the Golden Gate Quartet to perform at Constitution Hall. This time the Daughters of the Revolution do not object.

1941: Pearl Harbor, Hawaii, is attacked on December 7th by Japanese forces. On December 8th, the United States enters World War II.

1941: The Tuskegee Institute establishes its first pilot training program for blacks. The Tuskegee Airmen—black pilots who trained there—fight heroically for the United States in World War II.

Thomas Dorsey's new gospel sound did not immediately become popular among African Americans because his style was not accepted by many churches and his music was not recorded. However, gospel quartets—like the Golden Gate Quartet shown here—quickly became famous due to their recordings and radio play. Like barbershop quartets, black religious quartets sang in rich harmonies.

1931: Nine black youths are charged with raping two white women in Scottsboro, Alabama. Although there is little evidence, the southern jury sentences them to death. The Supreme Court overturns their convictions twice. In a third trial, four of the Scottsboro boys are freed; but five are sentenced to long prison terms.

1934: Harlem's famous Apollo Theater opens.

1934: In this year, eight gospel quartets record their music. By 1939, every major record label is recording at least one gospel quartet.

1936: African-American track star Jesse Owens wins four gold medals at the Berlin Olympics.

I see the rhythm of gospel women

hugging you, hugging me, hugging Him,
caring for our people, hearts filled to the brim.
(*When I grow up, I want to be just like them.*)
With sanctified voices—powerful and strong—
our gospel divas channel His love through song:

Queen Mahalia moves us up a little higher,
The Cotton Club finds Sister Tharpe in swing.
Pastor Shirley preaches with the choir,
shouting and telling stories before she starts to sing.

Gospel women turn city streets into sacred spaces,
recording studios into holy places.
They pull us up out of gutters and into the pews
to ease our burden and bring us good news,
mixing the message of salvation
with the rhythms of the blues.
Gospel women make music that shows
He's got the whole world in His hands,
turning our earthly sorrows
into hopes for the promised land.
I feel the loving rhythms of our gospel mothers
creating music that feels like home.

1948: Mahalia Jackson's "Move on Up a Little Higher" sells over two million copies, making her the Queen of Gospel.

1950: Mahalia Jackson brings gospel to Carnegie Hall. Her popularity increases as she is featured as one of the first African Americans on national television.

1950: Poet Gwendolyn Brooks becomes the first African American to win a Pulitzer Prize.

1955: While touring in South Carolina, Shirley Caesar's entourage stops at a gas station to buy drinks. Shirley's crew is attacked by the gas station owner and his attendants. Several members of her group are beaten with hammers and bottles. Shirley escapes unharmed.

1935: Mary McLeod Bethune, the daughter of slaves, founder of the Bethune-Cookman College, and advisor to President Roosevelt, starts the National Council of Negro Women, bringing together the leaders of twenty-eight women's organizations.

1938: Sister Rosetta Tharpe records four songs with Decca Records. Church members are shocked by her more secular style, but the public loves her. Tharpe becomes the first female crossover gospel artist and performs with swing bands in the 1940s.

1941-45: A second wave of southern blacks migrates north and west to provide labor for the war industry. Gospel singer Roebuck "Pops" Staples and his family are part of this movement. They move from Mississippi to Chicago to work in the meat-packing plants. The family later becomes the famous Staples Singers.

Black women have always been strong supporters of the black church. Despite the lack of opportunities in a world run by men, black women made their mark in America. In religious circles and in the larger entertainment world, there are many notable female gospel singers. This painting is a tribute to three of them: Mahalia Jackson, Sister Rosetta Tharpe, and Shirley Caesar.

23

get stronger as radio stations start to play

more and more of our music every day.

Gospel quartets and choirs—now much in demand—

travel from town to town to sing and shake hands

with the crowd.

I watch our famous singers, who perform to standing ovations,

get shuffled off to the colored sections of trains at the station.

"With these Jim Crow laws, we might as well be back on the plantation,"

Brother William grumbles with frustration.

(See, Brother William just got home from the war

and he—like other black men—were really pretty sore

that the country they fought for did not respect them more.)

So when gospel singers come to perform in our town,

Mama offers our home so they can rest, lie down,

and enjoy a good home-cooked meal (best cornbread around!).

I see the rhythm of the gospel highway

in the warm, grateful faces of the singers who show up at our door.

After World War II, many new record companies emerged, recording more gospel music. Gospel singers performed in churches, community centers, and auditoriums across the country. This network of venues was called the "gospel highway." Because of discrimination, blacks were not allowed to stay in most hotels or eat in most restaurants and had to travel in the poor third-class sections of trains and buses. The more successful singers traveled in their own buses and cars, but often encountered racism during their tours.

1945: World War II ends with the surrender of Germany and Japan.

1947: Jackie Robinson is signed to the Brooklyn Dodgers, becoming the first black man to play major league baseball.

1948: President Harry S. Truman issues an order to integrate the U.S. armed forces. Before this order, black and white American soldiers fought separately in segregated military units.

1950: African-American scholar and U. S. diplomat Ralph Bunche is the first person of color to win the Nobel Peace Prize for his work in negotiating an Arab-Israeli truce in Palestine.

1950: Sam Cooke joins the Soul Stirrers, pushing them to the top of their careers. Cooke goes on to become one of the most notable gospel singers to successfully cross over into secular music.

1954: In the case of *Brown v. Board of Education of Topeka, Kansas*, the Supreme Court rules that segregation in public schools is unconstitutional. After this ruling, schools start to become integrated. The case was argued and won by African-American attorney Thurgood Marshall.

I see the rhythm of Our Lament

as people of all races sing our discontent
through gospel's Freedom Songs.

The Staples demand, *"Respect yourself!"*

"That's enough," wails Dorothy Coates.

"People get ready," warns Curtis Mayfield
with his uplifting falsetto notes.

The voices of the people start to fly,
and *"We Shall Overcome"* becomes the movement's battle cry.
I see the passion of the students who come into our town
to convince us we must stand our ground.

"Register to vote, fight for your rights,
don't settle for less, get up and unite!"

My mother takes a deep breath, clears out her throat,
combs back her hair, puts on her coat,
and says, *"It's time, I'm registering to vote."*
My father, in silence, looks at her with pride,
then he puts on his hat and stands by her side,
and I watch them leave together, my eyes open wide.

I see the rhythm of the Freedom Songs and

I have a dream.

The Civil Rights Movement of the 1960s brought attention to the fact that, even a hundred years after slavery was outlawed, blacks were not yet treated as equal American citizens. Here black university students stage a "sit-in" at a Woolworth's lunch counter, peacefully protesting the fact that blacks cannot be served food there. Behind them, sanitation workers march for basic employment rights. The guards represent the National Guard troops who were sent by President Kennedy to protect the protesters. At the bottom, people are lined up to register to vote for the first time.

1955: A young black boy, Emmett Till, is brutally killed for allegedly whistling at a white woman in Mississippi. Two white men charged with his murder are acquitted by an all-white jury. They later boast about killing the boy. The public outrage helps the Civil Rights Movement.

1955: Rosa Parks is arrested for refusing to give up her bus seat to a white passenger. In response, Montgomery, Alabama's black community launches a successful year-long bus boycott.

1957: Although ordered by the Federal government to allow the students in, nine black youths are blocked from entering Central High School in Little Rock, Arkansas. Federal troops and the National Guard intervene on behalf of the students, who become known as the "Little Rock Nine."

1961: Over the spring and summer, 1,000 white and black student volunteers begin taking bus trips through the South to test new laws prohibiting segregation in bus and railway stations. They are called "freedom riders."

1963: President John F. Kennedy is assassinated.

1963: Dr. Martin Luther King Jr. delivers his famous "I Have a Dream" speech at the March on Washington for Jobs and Freedom, which is attended by about 250,000 people.

1963: The Sixteenth Street Baptist Church in Birmingham, Alabama, is bombed, killing four little girls.

1964: President Lyndon Johnson signs the Civil Rights Act, prohibiting discrimination of all kinds based on race, color, religion, or national origin.

1964: Dr. King receives the Nobel Peace Prize.

I see the rhythms of exploration,

a time of **open minds, fairer laws,** and **innovation.**

We put a man on the moon, up in outer space—

from where he stands he can see no face, no trace

of any single person—only one planet, one place.

But back on Earth that still is not the case.

(I wonder what it's like not to see race.)

I see riots in my city—too many drugs and guns.

Although we now have equal rights, there's still work to be done.

But ... on the TV and radio, there is an exciting change:

the rhythms of rock, pop, and soul combine, exchange,

and broaden the range of gospel music.

Bradford brings gospel to the Broadway stage.
Hawkins' "Oh Happy Day" becomes all the rage.
Crouch finds new audiences to engage.
Cleveland's foot-stompin' choir music comes of age.

These fathers of modern gospel create new voices so that

black, white, young, old now have choices of joyous, uplifting music.

1962: James Cleveland records "Peace Be Still" with the First Baptist Church Choir, which sells 800,000 copies. He becomes a superstar overnight.

1965—1970: Americans actively protest the United States' involvement in the Vietnam War.

1965: Congress passes the Voting Rights Act of 1965, making it easier for southern blacks to register to vote.

1965: In six days of rioting in Los Angeles, thirty-five people are killed and almost 1,000 injured.

1967: Major race riots also take place in Newark and Detroit.

1967: Attorney and civil rights leader Thurgood Marshall becomes the first black Supreme Court Justice.

1968: Dr. Martin Luther King Jr. is assassinated in Memphis, Tennessee.

1976: The Apple II computer is introduced, revolutionizing the personal home computer.

1975: Morehouse is established— the only black medical school in the United States.

In the 1960s and '70s, American culture started to reflect the diversity of its people. Black musical genres like rhythm and blues and soul became hugely popular all over the world. Gospel was also influenced by these styles of music—and the line between gospel and secular music became blurred. In the background of this picture, you can see the faces of some of the gospel innovators of this time (*from left to right*): Edwin Hawkins, Sam Cooke, James Cleveland, Thomas Dorsey, Andraé Crouch, Rance Allen, and Alex Bradford. The choir leader is James Cleveland, who developed the modern black gospel choir style.

I see the rhythm of Motown and funk

in the new pop-gospel music of our time.

The smoothness of the music makes us **sway to the beat,**

the bass lines make us want to jump to our feet,

and its popularity moves it from the church to the street.

Nana and the old folks complain every day:

> *"Real gospel music can't be sung that way.*
>
> *And gospel at the Apollo? Just ain't right," they'd say.*
>
> *"Gospel should have that old Dorsey feel."*

But to us **Al Green, Tramaine,** and the **Winans** were ideal.

I never understood why the old folks complained.

If the music spread the word, then it wasn't in vain.

Can't gospel music inspire and entertain?

Besides, the music was more fun than listening to them explain

how things were back in their day!

I see the rhythm of gospel soul reach out and speak

to a new generation.

There were many contemporary gospel stars in the 1980s, but one family is credited as being the biggest influence on gospel music in that decade—the Winans. Here, brother and sister BeBe (*right*) and CeCe Winans (*left*) are singing at Harlem's Apollo Theater. Over the course of the 1960s to the '80s, two branches of gospel music developed: contemporary gospel, which reached a wide secular audience, and traditional gospel, which was still extremely popular.

1981: James Cleveland becomes the first gospel artist to receive a star on Hollywood's Walk of Fame.

1983: Alice Walker wins the Pulitzer Prize for Fiction for her novel, *The Color Purple.*

1984: *The Cosby Show* debuts—the most successful TV series featuring an African-American cast in history.

1984: Civil rights activist Rev. Jesse Jackson runs for president of the United States.

1985: BeBe and CeCe Winans are the first black artists to sign with Christian record label, Sparrow Records.

1985: Youth minister Stephen Wiley releases the first full-length Christian rap album, *Bible Break.*

1986: January 20th is officially designated Martin Luther King Jr. Day, a national holiday.

1990 : South African activist Nelson Mandela is freed after spending twenty-seven years in prison for fighting against the racist apartheid laws of his country.

1991 : Gospel Music Association adds a rap/hip-hop album category to its Dove Music Awards.

1992 : The Los Angeles policemen on trial for the beating of an African-American man, Rodney King, are acquitted. The acquittal ignites civil disorder in communities of color in Los Angeles.

1992 : Dr. Mae Jemison becomes the first African-American woman in space.

1993 : Toni Morrison becomes the first African American to win the Nobel Prize in Literature for her novel, Beloved.

I see the rhythm of
GOSPEL MUSIC POWER

moving the word through television, internet, and radio,

and on the stages of our mega-churches where they echo and flow

into the hearts of thousands.

Donnie urges me to get up when I fall down.

Soulful Yolanda crafts her music with a slick, urban sound.

Kirk and the Family's crossover gospel is the best around.

Tye Tribbett takes chances and explores new ground.

(*I really like his more hip-hoppy sound.*)

We young people love the music, but it surely confounds

our elders.

Our singers are superstars; our ministers, celebrities.

The power of their performances makes us want to drop to our knees and pray,

Please! Help us in our journey to live a better way.

I hear the rhythm of my childhood plight

in music that helps me understand what's wrong, what's right,

that teaches me how to live a life that is contrite

and full of love that is divinely bright.

1994 : Nelson Mandela is elected the first black president of South Africa in the country's first free elections. Apartheid is officially over.

1995 : The Million Man March is organized in Washington, D. C., to affirm collective responsibility among African Americans and to protest the violence, drugs, and unemployment affecting black men.

1998 : The body of James Byrd Jr. is found. He was lynched in Jasper, Texas, by three white men.

The 1990s saw the rise of the black urban "mega-churches," where thousands of worshippers could gather for one service. The popularity of gospel music prompted the birth of a gospel music cable television station, magazine, and music awards, yet the message of the music continued to rise above the commercialism. New voices, such as that of Donnie McClurkin and Kirk Franklin, engaged many young people who were still negatively affected by poverty, drugs, broken families, poor schools, and the lack of social services.

I SEE THE RHYTHM of HOLY HIP-HOP

rise from the alleys and the urban underground,
  speaking to me with familiar sounds.

I see the rhythms reflecting my life,

my hopelessness, struggle, pain, and strife,
  trying to find meaning and purpose for my soul,
    a map for my journey, a hand up out of the hole.

But the world I see
on internet and TV
doesn't speak to me.

It is not my family's life of bounced rent checks
  or drugs and violence in the projects.
    The world just seems far too complex,
      and I don't have many choices.

Then I hear the holy message through the hip-hop rhythms,

those rappin' rhythms that release the tension,
  exposing painful memories I dare not mention,
    opening spaces in my heart to receive comprehension
      that there is a different life, a new dimension
        for people like me.

I see the rhythm and hope in hip-hop gospel,

and the rhythm lives on in me.

2001: On September 11th, al-Qaeda terrorists hijack and crash four commercial airplanes into the World Trade Center, the Pentagon, and a field in Pennsylvania, killing almost 3,000 people. This prompts President George W. Bush to declare a "War on Terrorism."

2001: African-Americans General Colin L. Powell and Condoleezza Rice are appointed to President Bush's cabinet. General Powell becomes secretary of state, and Condoleezza Rice becomes the president's chief of staff.

2003: In *Grutter v. Bollinger*, the Supreme Court rules that race can be one of the factors considered by colleges when selecting their students because it furthers "a compelling interest in obtaining the educational benefits that flow from a diverse student body."

2005: Hurricane Katrina devastates the Gulf Coast. The black communities are hit the hardest.

2008: African-American Illinois senator Barack Obama is elected the 44th president of the United States.

Like the blues, jazz, rhythm-and-blues, and soul styles of earlier years, hip-hop also influenced gospel. Cross Movement, Tye Tribbett, Lecrae, and Da T.R.U.T.H. are only a few of the many musicians who used rap and hip-hop styles to reach the youth of the 21st century with positive inspirational messages and stories of finding salvation through Jesus Christ.

the Word on Gospel

"...sometimes you feel something deep down inside you that has to come out—that's the way my gospel singing was for me. I felt I had to express it or be torn apart by it..."

—Mahalia Jackson, 1911—1972

"I've always had struggles but I didn't take them to heart and let them destroy me. I been thrown out of some of the best churches. If they were good ministerial men, they would have helped me... But I got out on my own and went on through the world with gospel and many, many people has been helped and saved by the gospel."

—Thomas A. Dorsey 1899—1999

"I was in need... there was a deficit in me... I remember falling to my knees and saying, 'God, forgive me.' And he did. And I'm here."

—Lecrae, 1980—

"It was a joyous sort of thing… it was a thing you patted your foot by. It wasn't a thing that made you want to cry, like 'my mama's dead and gone'… It was all light, really entertaining. And it had some merit, like in the narrative tunes, and a lot of people had never heard about all the Biblical heroes…"

—Willie Johnson of The Golden Gate Quartet, 1935–2001

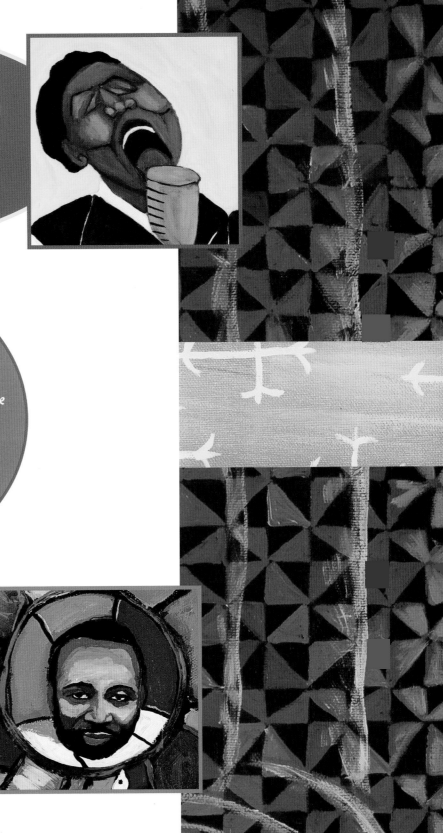

"I see contemporary gospel as being gospel with only the music changing, not the words. Anytime you've got a song and the Lord is not mentioned to the extent that it's going to help somebody, you're not listening to a gospel song."

—Shirley Caesar, 1938—

"Music has to have a concept of the Word in it, because the Word changes a situation. So I ask, who is the song about? What is the song talking about? Why are you talking about it? When did it happen and what went on? And why? What is God trying to tell you through this?…the storytelling is where the strength is."

—Andraé Crouch, 1947—

Discography

The bonus CD included in the back of this book features these five gospel songs representing different eras in African-American gospel history:

Gospel Quartets: "Wade in the Water"—Golden Gate Quartet

Gospel Women: "I Will Move on Up a Little Higher"—Mahalia Jackson

Gospel Soul (Motown and Funk): "Hallelujah Praise"—CeCe Winans

Gospel Power: "Jesus Be a Fence Around Me"—Fred Hammond and Radical for Christ

Holy Hip-Hop: "I Love You"—Cross Movement

Here are some of our other favorites. Listen to these as you start your exploration of gospel music.

Africa: "Ke Na Le Modisa"—Soweto Gospel Choir

New World—The Great Awakening: "Swing Low, Sweet Chariot" or "Nobody Knows the Trouble I Seen"—traditional gospel songs that have been sung by various artists

Plantation Sundays: "Run Old Jeremiah: Echoes of the Ring Shout"—you can find a good sample of a ring shout sung by Joe Washington Brown and Austin Coleman in 1934 at http://historymatters.gmu.edu/d/5759/

Our Hope—The Promised Land: "Go Down, Moses" or "Steal Away"—traditional gospel songs that have been sung by various artists

Jubilee Day: "I'm on the Battlefield for My Lord"—The Fisk Jubilee Singers

Sanctified Churches: "We'll Understand It Better By and By"—Charles Tindley

Bronzeville: "Take My Hand, Precious Lord"—Thomas Dorsey

Gospel Quartets: "Lord I've Tried"—Soul Stirrers; "Ezekiel Saw the Wheel"—Golden Gate Quartet

Gospel Women: "He's Got the Whole World in His Hands"—Mahalia Jackson; "Jesus, I Love Calling Your Name"—Shirley Caesar; "Didn't It Rain"—Rosetta Tharpe

Gospel Highway: "Jesus Gave Me Water"—Sam Cooke; "The Lord's Prayer"—Five Blind Boys of Mississippi

Our Lament—The Civil Rights Movement: "We Shall Overcome"—the American civil rights anthem

Exploration—Fathers of Modern Gospel: "Jesus is the Answer"—Andraé Crouch; "Oh Happy Day"—Edwin Hawkins; "Peace Be Still"—James Cleveland

Gospel Soul—Motown and Funk: "I'll Take You There"—BeBe and CeCe Winans; "Wherever You Are"—Yolanda Adams

Gospel Power: "Why We Sing"—Kirk Franklin; "Stand"—Donnie McClurkin; "No Way"—Tye Tribbett

Holy Hip-Hop: "Holy Culture"—Cross Movement; "Take Me As I Am"—Lecrae; "Who Am I?"—Da T.R.U.T.H.